Duino Elegies

Duino Elegies

Rainer Maria Rilke

A Bilingual Edition

Translated by
Dora Van Vranken and Roger Nicholson Pierce

The Center of Balance Press
2513 24th Avenue Longmont, CO 80503
arpierce1@mac.com

Library of Congress Control Number: 2010921739

ISBN: 9781879970038

Cover design by Gabrielle Rohmer
Cover image by Benjamin Pierce

for Krista and Nadine Van Vranken

and in loving memory of
Robert Lowell Pierce, Jr.

The translators wish to thank Ursula Berg-Lunk for her expert
comments on a range of language and syntactical questions.

Contents

Foreword

Translating asks for both fidelity to the original and grace in the receiving language. The tension between the two creates a spectrum of possibilities: at one extreme, strict attention to the details of the source and at the other a free play of the translator's own creativity in rendering the original. The numerous translations of the *Duino Elegies* into English are spread all across this broad spectrum. Those who lean toward freedom may point to the danger that scrupulous attention to fine points will produce a crabbed, un-English poem; those who focus on fidelity will claim that they are giving the English reader an unadulterated experience of the original.

We have found that being as literal as possible has been a dependable and stimulating pathway from German into English—from Rilke's often idiosyncratic, sometimes ambiguous, highly metaphorical German into an English version that preserves these values. Of course we have carried out this conservative impulse by giving close attention to the denotations of his words—but also to his artistry with such elements as leitmotif, syntax, metaphor, ambiguity, rhythm, and tone of voice. Incidentally, Rilke's standard of accuracy in translation, whether in his own practice or in that of others, would place him at the conservative end of this spectrum.

The *Translation Notes* at the end of this book (page 85) discuss some of our translating principles in more detail.

Duineser Elegien

aus dem Besitz der Fürstin
Marie von Thurn und Taxis-Hohenlohe

Duino Elegies

from the property of Princess
Marie von Thurn und Taxis-Hohenlohe

Die Erste Elegie

Wer, wenn ich schriee, hörte mich denn aus der Engel
Ordnungen? und gesetzt selbst, es nähme
einer mich plötzlich ans Herz: ich verginge von seinem
stärkeren Dasein. Denn das Schöne ist nichts
als des Schrecklichen Anfang, den wir noch grade ertragen,   5
und wir bewundern es so, weil es gelassen verschmäht,
uns zu zerstören. Ein jeder Engel ist schrecklich.
   Und so verhalt ich mich denn und verschlucke den Lockruf
dunkelen Schluchzens. Ach, wen vermögen
wir denn zu brauchen? Engel nicht, Menschen nicht,   10
und die findigen Tiere merken es schon,
daß wir nicht sehr verläßlich zuhaus sind
in der gedeuteten Welt. Es bleibt uns vielleicht
irgend ein Baum an dem Abhang, daß wir ihn täglich
wiedersähen; es bleibt uns die Straße von gestern   15
und das verzogene Treusein einer Gewohnheit,
der es bei uns gefiel, und so blieb sie und ging nicht.
   O und die Nacht, die Nacht, wenn der Wind voller Weltraum
uns am Angesicht zehrt —, wem bliebe sie nicht, die ersehnte,
sanft enttäuschende, welche dem einzelnen Herzen   20
mühsam bevorsteht. Ist sie den Liebenden leichter?
Ach, sie verdecken sich nur mit einander ihr Los.
   Weißt du's *noch* nicht? Wirf aus den Armen die Leere

The First Elegy

Who, if I cried out, would ever hear me among the angels'
orders? and even if one suddenly
took me to his heart: I'd dissolve in his
stronger being. For the beautiful is nothing
but terror's beginning, which we just barely endure,
and we admire it so because it calmly disdains
to destroy us. Every angel is terrible.
  And so I hold myself back and choke down the alluring call
of my dark sobbing. Ah, then whom can
we need? Not angels, not men,
and the shrewd animals no doubt notice
that we're not so securely at home
in our interpreted world. There stays for us maybe
some tree on the slope that we'd see
day by day; yesterday's street stays for us,
and the indulged loyalty of a habit
that liked us, and so it stayed and didn't leave.
  Oh and the night, the night, when the wind full of world-space
gnaws on our faces —, for whom would she not stay, the longed for,
gently disappointing night, which awaits
the weary solitary heart. Is she easier for the lovers?
Ah, with each other they only conceal their fate.
  You *still* don't know it? Fling the emptiness from your arms

zu den Räumen hinzu, die wir atmen; vielleicht daß die Vögel
die erweiterte Luft fühlen mit innigerm Flug.   25

Ja, die Frühlinge brauchten dich wohl. Es muteten manche
Sterne dir zu, daß du sie spürtest. Es hob
sich eine Woge heran im Vergangenen, oder
da du vorüberkamst am geöffneten Fenster,
gab eine Geige sich hin. Das alles war Auftrag.   30
Aber bewältigtest du's? Warst du nicht immer
noch von Erwartung zerstreut, als kündigte alles
eine Geliebte dir an? (Wo willst du sie bergen,
da doch die großen fremden Gedanken bei dir
aus und ein gehn und öfters bleiben bei Nacht.)   35
Sehnt es dich aber, so singe die Liebenden; lange
noch nicht unsterblich genug ist ihr berühmtes Gefühl.
Jene, du neidest sie fast, Verlassenen, die du
so viel liebender fandst als die Gestillten. Beginn
immer von neuem die nie zu erreichende Preisung;   40
denk: es erhält sich der Held, selbst der Untergang war ihm
nur ein Vorwand, zu sein: seine letzte Geburt.
Aber die Liebenden nimmt die erschöpfte Natur
in sich zurück, als wären nicht zweimal die Kräfte,
dieses zu leisten. Hast du der Gaspara Stampa   45
denn genügend gedacht, daß irgend ein Mädchen,
dem der Geliebte entging, am gesteigerten Beispiel
dieser Liebenden fühlt: daß ich würde wie sie?

into the spaces we breathe; perhaps so the birds
will feel the widened air with more fervent flying.

Yes, the springtimes must have needed you. Many a star
demanded your attention. A wave of things past
lifted itself toward you, or
as you came by an opened window
a violin bestowed itself. All that was a mission.
But did you accomplish it? Weren't you still
distracted by expectation, as though everything were announcing
a beloved to you? (Where will you shelter her,
since those great strange thoughts
go in and out and sometimes stay the night?)
But when you are filled with longing, sing of the lovers;
not nearly immortal enough is their celebrated feeling.
Those, you almost envy them, the deserted ones, whom you
found so much more loving than the satisfied ones. Begin
always anew the never attainable praising;
think: the hero prevails, even his downfall was
only his pretext to be: his final birth.
But exhausted nature takes the lovers
back into herself, as if there weren't the strength
to achieve this twice. Have you given enough thought
to Gaspara Stampa, so that some young girl, abandoned
by her lover, would feel from the heightened example
of this loving woman: oh, to be like her?

Sollen nicht endlich uns diese ältesten Schmerzen
fruchtbarer werden? Ist es nicht Zeit, daß wir liebend   50
uns vom Geliebten befrein und es bebend bestehn:
wie der Pfeil die Sehne besteht, um gesammelt im Absprung
mehr zu sein als er selbst. Denn Bleiben ist nirgends.

Stimmen, Stimmen. Höre, mein Herz, wie sonst nur
Heilige hörten: daß sie der riesige Ruf   55
aufhob vom Boden; sie aber knieten,
Unmögliche, weiter und achtetens nicht:
So waren sie hörend. Nicht, daß du *Gottes* ertrügest
die Stimme, bei weitem. Aber das Wehende höre,
die ununterbrochene Nachricht, die aus Stille sich bildet.   60
Es rauscht jetzt von jenen jungen Toten zu dir.
Wo immer du eintratst, redete nicht in Kirchen
zu Rom und Neapel ruhig ihr Schicksal dich an?
Oder es trug eine Inschrift sich erhaben dir auf,
wie neulich die Tafel in Santa Maria Formosa.   65
Was sie mir wollen? leise soll ich des Unrechts
Anschein abtun, der ihrer Geister
reine Bewegung manchmal ein wenig behindert.

Freilich ist es seltsam, die Erde nicht mehr zu bewohnen,
kaum erlernte Gebräuche nicht mehr zu üben,   70
Rosen, und andern eigens versprechenden Dingen,
nicht die Bedeutung menschlicher Zukunft zu geben;
das, was man war in unendlich ängstlichen Händen,

Shouldn't these oldest sorrows finally
become more fruitful for us? Isn't it time to lovingly
free ourselves from the beloved and, trembling, to endure it:
the way the arrow endures the string so as to be, collected in the leap,
more than itself. For staying is nowhere.

Voices, voices. Listen, my heart, as usually only
saints have listened: so that the immense call
lifted them off the ground; but they knelt on,
impossible ones, and didn't heed it:
so were they listening. Not that you could bear *God's*
voice, far from it. But listen to the wafting,
the incessant message that shapes itself from the stillness.
It murmurs toward you now from those young dead.
Wherever you entered, in churches of Rome and Naples,
didn't their destiny speak softly to you?
Or a sublime inscription entrusted itself to you,
as lately the tablet in Santa Maria Formosa.
What do they want from me? Quietly I'm to remove
the appearance of wrong that sometimes slightly hinders
the pure movement of their spirits.

Of course it is strange to inhabit the earth no longer,
to practice no longer the barely learned customs,
not to give roses and other especially promising things
the meaning of a human future;
no longer to be what one was

nicht mehr zu sein, und selbst den eigenen Namen
wegzulassen wie ein zerbrochenes Spielzeug.   75
Seltsam, die Wünsche nicht weiterzuwünschen. Seltsam,
alles, was sich bezog, so lose im Raume
flattern zu sehen. Und das Totsein ist mühsam
und voller Nachholn, daß man allmählich ein wenig
Ewigkeit spürt. — Aber Lebendige machen   80
alle den Fehler, daß sie zu stark unterscheiden.
Engel (sagt man) wüßten oft nicht, ob sie unter
Lebenden gehn oder Toten. Die ewige Strömung
reißt durch beide Bereiche alle Alter
immer mit sich und übertönt sie in beiden.   85

    Schließlich brauchen sie uns nicht mehr, die Früheentrückten,
man entwöhnt sich des Irdischen sanft, wie man den Brüsten
milde der Mutter entwächst. Aber wir, die so große
Geheimnisse brauchen, denen aus Trauer so oft
seliger Fortschritt entspringt —: könnten wir sein ohne sie?   90
Ist die Sage umsonst, daß einst in der Klage um Linos
wagende erste Musik dürre Erstarrung durchdrang;
daß erst im erschrockenen Raum, dem ein beinah göttlicher Jüngling
plötzlich für immer enttrat, das Leere in jene
Schwingung geriet, die uns jetzt hinreißt und tröstet und hilft.   95

in infinitely anxious hands, and even put aside
one's own name, like a broken toy.
Strange not to go on desiring our desires. Strange
to see all that once was interconnected
fluttering so loosely in space. And being dead is toilsome
and full of retrieving, so one can gradually
feel a little eternity. — But the living all make
the mistake of distinguishing too sharply.
Angels (they say) often don't know if they're walking
among the living or the dead. The eternal current
through both domains sweeps all ages
along with it forever, and overpowers them in both.

    In the end they no longer need us, the early-departed,
softly one weans oneself from the earthly the way one gently
outgrows the breasts of the mother. But we, who need
such great mysteries, for whom blessed advances
so often spring from mourning —: *could* we exist without them?
Is the legend for nothing that once, in the lament for Linos,
daring first music thrust through barren numbness;
that in the startled space which an almost godlike youth
had suddenly left forever, the emptiness first fell into that
vibration which now enraptures and consoles and helps us.

Die Zweite Elegie

Jeder Engel ist schrecklich. Und dennoch, weh mir,
ansing ich euch, fast tödliche Vögel der Seele,
wissend um euch. Wohin sind die Tage Tobiae,
da der Strahlendsten einer stand an der einfachen Haustür,
zur Reise ein wenig verkleidet und schon nicht mehr furchtbar;   5
(Jüngling dem Jüngling, wie er neugierig hinaussah).
Träte der Erzengel jetzt, der gefährliche, hinter den Sternen
eines Schrittes nur nieder und herwärts: hochauf-
schlagend erschlüg uns das eigene Herz. Wer seid ihr?

Frühe Gcglückte, ihr Verwöhnten der Schöpfung,   10
Höhenzüge, morgenrötliche Grate
aller Erschaffung, — Pollen der blühenden Gottheit,
Gelenke des Lichtes, Gänge, Treppen, Throne,
Räume aus Wesen, Schilde aus Wonne, Tumulte
stürmisch entzückten Gefühls und plötzlich, einzeln,   15
Spiegel: die die entströmte eigene Schönheit
wiederschöpfen zurück in das eigene Antlitz.

Denn wir, wo wir fühlen, verflüchtigen; ach wir
atmen uns aus und dahin; von Holzglut zu Holzglut
geben wir schwächern Geruch. Da sagt uns wohl einer: 20
ja, du gehst mir ins Blut, dieses Zimmer, der Frühling
füllt sich mit dir . . . Was hilfts, er kann uns nicht halten,
wir schwinden in ihm und um ihn. Und jene, die schön sind,

12

The Second Elegy

Every angel is terrible. And yet, alas,
I sing unto you, almost deadly birds of the soul,
knowing about you. Where have they gone, the days of Tobias,
when one of the most radiant stood at the simple door,
a little disguised for the journey and already no longer alarming;
(a youth to the youth as he looked out curiously).
If the archangel now—the dangerous one—from behind the stars,
took just one step down and toward us: high-
beating, our own heart would beat us dead. Who are you?

Early successes, you pampered ones of creation,
high ranges, morning-red ridges of
all creation, — pollen of the blossoming Godhead,
joints of light, corridors, stairways, thrones,
spaces made of being, shields made of ecstasy, turmoils of
stormy-enraptured feeling and suddenly, singly,
mirrors: that scoop their own outstreamed beauty
back into their own face again.

For we, when we feel, evaporate; ah, we
breathe ourselves out and away; from ember to ember
we give off a weaker scent. True, someone might say to us:
yes, you seep into my blood, this room, the springtime
fills itself with you . . . It can't be helped, he can't hold us,
we vanish in and around him. And those who are beautiful,

o wer hält sie zurück? Unaufhörlich steht Anschein
auf in ihrem Gesicht und geht fort. Wie Tau von dem Frühgras   25
hebt sich das Unsre von uns, wie die Hitze von einem
heißen Gericht. O Lächeln, wohin? O Aufschaun:
neue, warme, entgehende Welle des Herzens —;
weh mir: wir *sinds* doch. Schmeckt denn der Weltraum,
in den wir uns lösen, nach uns? Fangen die Engel   30
wirklich nur Ihriges auf, ihnen Entströmtes,
oder ist manchmal, wie aus Versehen, ein wenig
unseres Wesens dabei? Sind wir in ihre
Züge soviel nur gemischt wie das Vage in die Gesichter
schwangerer Frauen? Sie merken es nicht in dem Wirbel   35
ihrer Rückkehr zu sich. (Wie sollten sie's merken.)

Liebende könnten, verstünden sie's, in der Nachtluft
wunderlich reden. Denn es scheint, daß uns alles
verheimlicht. Siehe, die Bäume *sind*; die Häuser,
die wir bewohnen, bestehn noch. Wir nur   40
ziehen allem vorbei wie ein luftiger Austausch.
Und alles ist einig, uns zu verschweigen, halb als
Schande vielleicht und halb als unsägliche Hoffnung.

Liebende, euch, ihr in einander Genügten,
frag ich nach uns. Ihr greift euch. Habt ihr Beweise?   45
Seht, mir geschiehts, daß meine Hände einander
inne werden oder daß mein gebrauchtes
Gesicht in ihnen sich schont. Das gibt mir ein wenig

14

oh, who holds them back? Unceasingly, appearance rises
in their faces and departs. Like dew from the morning grass
what's ours rises from us, like the heat from
a hot dish. Oh smile, where to? Oh upward look:
new, warm, escaping wave of the heart —;
Alas, we *are* that. Does then world-space taste of us
when we dissolve in it? Do the angels really capture
only what's theirs, their outstreamed radiance,
or is sometimes, as though by mistake, a little
of our essence in it? Are we mixed
into their features only as much as the vagueness in faces
of pregnant women? They do not notice it in the whirl
of their return to themselves. (How could they notice it.)

Lovers could, if they only knew how, speak wondrously
in the night air. For it seems that everything
keeps us a secret. See, the trees *are*; the houses
we inhabit still exist. We alone
flow past everything like a breezy barter.
And everything agrees to be silent about us, half
from shame perhaps, and half from unspeakable hope.

Lovers, you, fulfilled in one another,
I ask about us. You grasp each other. Do you have proof?
See, it happens to me that my hands
become aware of each other or that my worn
face shelters itself in them. That gives me a slight

Empfindung. Doch wer wagte darum schon zu *sein*?
Ihr aber, die ihr im Entzücken des anderen   50
zunehmt, bis er euch überwältigt
anfleht: nicht *mehr* —; die ihr unter den Händen
euch reichlicher werdet wie Traubenjahre;
die ihr manchmal vergeht, nur weil der andre
ganz überhand nimmt: euch frag ich nach uns. Ich weiß,   55
ihr berührt euch so selig, weil die Liebkosung verhält,
weil die Stelle nicht schwindet, die ihr, Zärtliche,
zudeckt; weil ihr darunter das reine
Dauern verspürt. So versprecht ihr euch Ewigkeit fast
von der Umarmung. Und doch, wenn ihr der ersten   60
Blicke Schrecken besteht und die Sehnsucht am Fenster,
und den ersten gemeinsamen Gang, *ein* Mal durch den Garten:
Liebende, *seid* ihrs dann noch? Wenn ihr einer dem andern
euch an den Mund hebt und ansetzt —: Getränk an Getränk:
o wie entgeht dann der Trinkende seltsam der Handlung.   65

Erstaunte euch nicht auf attischen Stelen die Vorsicht
menschlicher Geste? war nicht Liebe und Abschied
so leicht auf die Schultern gelegt, als wär es aus anderm
Stoffe gemacht als bei uns? Gedenkt euch der Hände,
wie sie drucklos beruhen, obwohl in den Torsen die Kraft steht. 70
Diese Beherrschten wußten damit: so weit sind wirs,
dieses ist unser, uns *so* zu berühren; stärker
stemmen die Götter uns an. Doch dies ist Sache der Götter.

sensation. But who would dare, for this alone, to *be*?
You, however, who grow in the rapture of the other,
until, overwhelmed, he begs you:
no *more* —; you who under those hands
become more abundant, like a bountiful vintage;
you who sometimes fade away just because the other
takes the upper hand completely: I ask you about us. I know,
you touch each other so blissfully because the caress lasts,
because the place doesn't vanish which you, tender ones,
cover; because you feel beneath it pure
duration. So you promise yourselves eternity almost
from the embrace. And yet, when you withstand
the terror of the first glances and the longing at the window
and the first walk together, *one* time through the garden:
lovers, is that still what you *are*? When you lift yourself
each to the other's mouth and set to —: drink for drink:
oh then how the drinker strangely eludes the act.

Were you not astonished by the caution of human gestures
on Attic stelae? was not love and parting
so lightly laid on their shoulders, as if it were made from
different stuff than ours? Think of their hands,
how they rest without pressure, though power lives in their torsos.
By this these self-ruled ones knew: this is our limit,
this is ours, *so* to touch one another; the gods
push harder against us. But that's the concern of the gods.

Fänden auch wir ein reines, verhaltenes, schmales
Menschliches, einen unseren Streifen Fruchtlands   75
zwischen Strom und Gestein. Denn das eigene Herz übersteigt uns
noch immer wie jene. Und wir können ihm nicht mehr
nachschaun in Bilder, die es besänftigen, noch in
göttliche Körper, in denen es größer sich mäßigt.

If only we also could find a pure, contained, narrow
humanness, a strip of fruitland of our own
between river and rock. For our own heart transcends us
still, as theirs did. And no longer can we
look back at it in images that calm it, nor in
godlike bodies where it more nobly tempers itself.

Die Dritte Elegie

Eines ist, die Geliebte zu singen. Ein anderes, wehe,
jenen verborgenen schuldigen Fluß-Gott des Bluts.
Den sie von weitem erkennt, ihren Jüngling, was weiß er
selbst von dem Herren der Lust, der aus dem Einsamen oft,
ehe das Mädchen noch linderte, oft auch als wäre sie nicht,   5
ach, von welchem Unkenntlichen triefend, das Gotthaupt
aufhob, aufrufend die Nacht zu unendlichem Aufruhr.
O des Blutes Neptun, o sein furchtbarer Dreizack.
O der dunkele Wind seiner Brust aus gewundener Muschel.
Horch, wie die Nacht sich muldet und höhlt. Ihr Sterne,   10
stammt nicht von euch des Liebenden Lust zu dem Antlitz
seiner Geliebten? Hat er die innige Einsicht
in ihr reines Gesicht nicht aus dem reinen Gestirn?

Du nicht hast ihm, wehe, nicht seine Mutter
hat ihm die Bogen der Braun so zur Erwartung gespannt.   15
Nicht an dir, ihn fühlendes Mädchen, an dir nicht
bog seine Lippe sich zum fruchtbarern Ausdruck.
Meinst du wirklich, ihn hätte dein leichter Auftritt
also erschüttert, du, die wandelt wie Frühwind?
Zwar du erschrakst ihm das Herz; doch ältere Schrecken   20
stürzten in ihn bei dem berührenden Anstoß.
Ruf ihn . . . du rufst ihn nicht ganz aus dunkelem Umgang.
Freilich, er *will*, er entspringt; erleichtert gewöhnt er
sich in dein heimliches Herz und nimmt und beginnt sich.

The Third Elegy

It is one thing to sing the beloved. Another, alas,
to sing that hidden guilty river-god of the blood.
The one she knows from afar, her young man, what does he know
himself of the Lord of Lust, who often from his solitude,
before the girl could soothe, often as though she didn't exist,
ah, dripping with what unknown, lifted
his godhead, calling up the night to endless uproar.
Oh the blood's Neptune, oh his dreadful trident.
Oh the dark wind of his breast from the twisted conch.
Listen, how the night grooves and hollows itself. You stars,
does it not come from you, the lover's desire
for the face of his beloved? Did not the pure constellations
give him his tender insight into her pure face?

Not you, alas, nor his mother,
has spanned the arches of his brows to such anticipation.
Not on you, girl who feels him, not on you did his lips
arch themselves to more fruitful expression.
Do you really believe that your light step would have
shaken him so, you who walk like the morning breeze?
True, you frightened his heart; but older fears
plunged into him with the impetus of your touch.
Call him . . . you won't quite call him from that dark company.
Of course he *wants to*, he escapes; relieved, he settles
into the home of your heart, and takes and begins himself.

21

Aber begann er sich je? 25
Mutter, *du* machtest ihn klein, du warsts, die ihn anfing;
dir war er neu, du beugtest über die neuen
Augen die freundliche Welt und wehrtest der fremden.
Wo, ach, hin sind die Jahre, da du ihm einfach
mit der schlanken Gestalt wallendes Chaos vertratst? 30
Vieles verbargst du ihm so; das nächtlich-verdächtige Zimmer
machtest du harmlos, aus deinem Herzen voll Zuflucht
mischtest du menschlichern Raum seinem Nacht-Raum hinzu.
Nicht in die Finsternis, nein, in dein näheres Dasein
hast du das Nachtlicht gestellt, und es schien wie aus Freundschaft. 35
Nirgends ein Knistern, das du nicht lächelnd erklärtest,
so als wüßtest du längst, *wann* sich die Diele benimmt . . .
Und er horchte und linderte sich. So vieles vermochte
zärtlich dein Aufstehn; hinter den Schrank trat
hoch im Mantel sein Schicksal, und in die Falten des Vorhangs 40
paßte, die leicht sich verschob, seine unruhige Zukunft.

Und er selbst, wie er lag, der Erleichterte, unter
schläfernden Lidern deiner leichten Gestaltung
Süße lösend in den gekosteten Vorschlaf —:
schien ein Gehüteter . . . Aber *innen*: wer wehrte, 45
hinderte innen in ihm die Fluten der Herkunft?
Ach, da *war* keine Vorsicht im Schlafenden; schlafend,
aber träumend, aber in Fiebern: wie er sich ein-ließ.
Er, der Neue, Scheuende, wie er verstrickt war,
mit des innern Geschehns weiterschlagenden Ranken 50

But did he ever begin himself?
Mother, *you* made him small, it was you who began him;
to you he was new, you bent over his new eyes
the friendly world, and warded off the alien.
Where, oh, have the years gone, when with your slender form
you simply blocked out surging chaos for him?
Many things you hid from him so; the night-blighted room
you made harmless; from your heart full of refuge
you added human space to his night-space.
Not in the darkness, no, in your nearer presence,
you placed the night light, and it shone as though in friendship.
Nowhere a creaking you didn't explain with a smile,
as if you always knew when the floor would misbehave . . .
And he listened and was soothed. Your rising tenderly
could do so much; tall in its cloak, his destiny
stepped behind the wardrobe; and his restless future,
shifting lightly, fit itself to the folds of the curtain.

And he himself, as he lay, the relieved one,
under drowsy lids, the sweetness of your gentle creation
dissolving into the first taste of sleep —:
seemed one protected . . . But *within*: who warded off,
hindered inside him, the floods of his forebears?
Ah, there *was* no caution in the sleeper; sleeping,
but dreaming, but in a fever: how he ventured in.
He, the new, the reluctant, how he was entangled
in the spreading tendrils of these inner events,

23

schon zu Mustern verschlungen, zu würgendem Wachstum, zu tierhaft
jagenden Formen. Wie er sich hingab —. Liebte.
Liebte sein Inneres, seines Inneren Wildnis,
diesen Urwald in ihm, auf dessen stummem Gestürztsein
lichtgrün sein Herz stand. Liebte. Verließ es, ging die   55
eigenen Wurzeln hinaus in gewaltigen Ursprung,
wo seine kleine Geburt schon überlebt war. Liebend
stieg er hinab in das ältere Blut, in die Schluchten,
wo das Furchtbare lag, noch satt von den Vätern. Und jedes
Schreckliche kannte ihn, blinzelte, war wie verständigt.   60
Ja, das Entsetzliche lächelte . . . Selten
hast du so zärtlich gelächelt, Mutter. Wie sollte
er es nicht lieben, da es ihm lächelte. *Vor* dir
hat ers geliebt, denn, da du ihn trugst schon,
war es im Wasser gelöst, das den Keimenden leicht macht.   65

Siehe, wir lieben nicht, wie die Blumen, aus einem
einzigen Jahr; uns steigt, wo wir lieben,
unvordenklicher Saft in die Arme. O Mädchen,
dies: daß wir liebten *in* uns, nicht Eines, ein Künftiges, sondern
das zahllos Brauende; nicht ein einzelnes Kind,   70
sondern die Väter, die wie Trümmer Gebirgs
uns im Grunde beruhn; sondern das trockene Flußbett
einstiger Mütter —; sondern die ganze
lautlose Landschaft unter dem wolkigen oder
reinen Verhängnis —: *dies* kam dir, Mädchen, zuvor.   75

already twisted into patterns, into strangling growth, into the shapes
of hunting animals. How he surrendered —. Loved.
Loved his interior, his interior's wilderness,
this primal forest inside him, on whose silent ruins,
light green, his own heart stood. Loved. Left it, went through
his own roots out into the mighty source,
where his small birth was already outlived. Loving,
he descended into the older blood, into the gorges
where the horrible lay, still glutted on the fathers. And every
terror recognized him, winked, was as if informed.
Yes, the appalling smiled . . . Seldom
have you smiled so tenderly, mother. How could
he not love it, since it smiled at him so. *Before* you
he loved it; for already, while you carried him,
it was dissolved in the water that makes the embryo light.

See, we do not love, like the flowers, from one
year only; for us, when we love,
immemorial sap rises into our arms. Oh girl,
this: that we loved *within* us not one, a future one, but
the whole ferment; not a single child,
but the fathers, who like mountain rubble
lie motionless in our depths —; but the dry river bed
of former mothers —; but the whole
soundless landscape under the cloudy or
clear doom —: *this* came, girl, before you.

Und du selber, was weißt du —, du locktest
Vorzeit empor in dem Liebenden. Welche Gefühle
wühlten herauf aus entwandelten Wesen. Welche
Frauen haßten dich da. Was für finstere Männer
regtest du auf im Geäder des Jünglings? Tote   80
Kinder wollten zu dir . . . O leise, leise,
tu ein liebes vor ihm, ein verläßliches Tagwerk, — führ ihn
nah an den Garten heran, gib ihm der Nächte
Übergewicht . . . . . .
           Verhalt ihn   85

And you yourself, what do you know —, you tempted
primal ages to rise in your beloved. What feelings
wallowed up from departed beings. What
women hated you there. What sort of grim men
did you stir in the veins of the youth? Dead
children reached for you . . . Oh softly, softly, let him see you
do a loving deed, a dependable day's work, — lead him
close to the garden, give him what outweighs
the nights . . . . . .

                Hold him back . . . . . .

Die Vierte Elegie

O Bäume Lebens, o wann winterlich?
Wir sind nicht einig. Sind nicht wie die Zug-
vögel verständigt. Überholt und spät,
so drängen wir uns plötzlich Winden auf
und fallen ein auf teilnahmslosen Teich.   5
Blühn und verdorrn ist uns zugleich bewußt.
Und irgendwo gehn Löwen noch und wissen,
solang sie herrlich sind, von keiner Ohnmacht.

Uns aber, wo wir Eines meinen, ganz,
ist schon des andern Aufwand fühlbar. Feindschaft   10
ist uns das Nächste. Treten Liebende
nicht immerfort an Ränder, eins im andern,
die sich versprachen Weite, Jagd und Heimat.
    Da wird für eines Augenblickes Zeichnung
ein Grund von Gegenteil bereitet, mühsam,   15
daß wir sie sähen; denn man ist sehr deutlich
mit uns. Wir kennen den Kontur
des Fühlens nicht: nur, was ihn formt von außen.
    Wer saß nicht bang vor seines Herzens Vorhang?
Der schlug sich auf: die Szenerie war Abschied.   20
Leicht zu verstehen. Der bekannte Garten,
und schwankte leise: dann erst kam der Tänzer.
Nicht *der*. Genug! Und wenn er auch so leicht tut,
er ist verkleidet und er wird ein Bürger

28

The Fourth Elegy

O trees of life, o when wintry?
We're not in harmony. Are not, like the migratory
birds, informed. Overtaken and late,
we thrust ourselves suddenly on winds
and fall on an uncaring pond.
Blossoming and withering: we're conscious of both at once.
And somewhere lions still roam, and know of no
weakness, while they are splendid.

But for us, while intending one thing, entirely,
the demands of the other are already felt. Discord
is closest to us. Do not lovers constantly
encounter boundaries, each in the other,
they who promised each other expanse, hunt, and home.
    So for the outline of a single moment,
a contrasting background is prepared, laboriously,
so we would see it; for they are very clear
with us. We don't know the contour of our
feeling: only what shapes it from outside.
    Who hasn't sat in fear before his heart's curtain?
It opened: the scene was parting.
Easy to understand. The familiar garden,
and swayed a little: only then came the dancer.
Not *him*. Enough! And even though he steps so lightly,
he's costumed and turns out bourgeois

und geht durch seine Küche in die Wohnung. 25
  Ich will nicht diese halbgefüllten Masken,
lieber die Puppe. Die ist voll. Ich will
den Balg aushalten und den Draht und ihr
Gesicht aus Aussehn. Hier. Ich bin davor.
Wenn auch die Lampen ausgehn, wenn mir auch 30
gesagt wird: Nichts mehr —, wenn auch von der Bühne
das Leere herkommt mit dem grauen Luftzug,
wenn auch von meinen stillen Vorfahrn keiner
mehr mit mir dasitzt, keine Frau, sogar
der Knabe nicht mehr mit dem braunen Schielaug: 35
Ich bleibe dennoch. Es gibt immer Zuschaun.

Hab ich nicht recht? Du, der um mich so bitter
das Leben schmeckte, meines kostend, Vater,
den ersten trüben Aufguß meines Müssens,
da ich heranwuchs, immer wieder kostend 40
und, mit dem Nachgeschmack so fremder Zukunft
beschäftigt, prüftest mein beschlagnes Aufschaun, —
der du, mein Vater, seit du tot bist, oft
in meiner Hoffnung, innen in mir, Angst hast,
und Gleichmut, wie ihn Tote haben, Reiche 45
von Gleichmut, aufgibst für mein bißchen Schicksal,
hab ich nicht recht? Und ihr, hab ich nicht recht,
die ihr mich liebtet für den kleinen Anfang
Liebe zu euch, von dem ich immer abkam,
weil mir der Raum in eurem Angesicht, 50

and enters his apartment through the kitchen.

　　I do not want these half-filled masks,
better the puppet. It's whole. I can bear
the stuffed body and the wire and its
make-believe face. Here. I'm facing it.
Even when the lights go out, even when I'm
told: That's all —, even when only emptiness
comes from the stage with the gray draft,
even when none of my silent forebears
still sits here with me, no woman, not even
the boy with the brown squint-eye any more:
I stay nonetheless. There's always watching.

Am I not right? You, whose life because of me
tasted so bitter, sampling mine, father,
the first murky outflow of my compulsion,
as I was growing up, again and again sampling,
and, engrossed in the aftertaste of so strange
a future, searched my clouded upturned look, —
you, my father, who, since your death, often
in my hope, inside me, are afraid,
and relinquish serenity such as the dead have,
realms of serenity, for my bit of destiny,
am I not right? And all you, am I not right,
you who loved me for my slight beginning
of love for you, from which I always strayed
because for me the space in your features,

31

da ich ihn liebte, überging in Weltraum,
in dem ihr nicht mehr wart . . . . : wenn mir zumut ist,
zu warten vor der Puppenbühne, nein,
so völlig hinzuschaun, daß, um mein Schauen
am Ende aufzuwiegen, dort als Spieler   55
ein Engel hinmuß, der die Bälge hochreißt.
Engel und Puppe: dann ist endlich Schauspiel.
Dann kommt zusammen, was wir immerfort
entzwein, indem wir da sind. Dann entsteht
aus unsern Jahreszeiten erst der Umkreis   60
des ganzen Wandelns. Über uns hinüber
spielt dann der Engel.   Sieh, die Sterbenden,
sollten sie nicht vermuten, wie voll Vorwand
das alles ist, was wir hier leisten. Alles
ist nicht es selbst. O Stunden in der Kindheit,   65
da hinter den Figuren mehr als nur
Vergangnes war und vor uns nicht die Zukunft.
Wir wuchsen freilich und wir drängten manchmal,
bald groß zu werden, denen halb zulieb,
die andres nicht mehr hatten, als das Großsein.   70
Und waren doch, in unserem Alleingehn,
mit Dauerndem vergnügt und standen da
im Zwischenraume zwischen Welt und Spielzeug,
an einer Stelle, die seit Anbeginn
gegründet war für einen reinen Vorgang.   75

Wer zeigt ein Kind, so wie es steht? Wer stellt

since I loved it, turned into world-space
where you no longer were . . . . : when I feel inclined
to wait before the puppet stage, no,
to look at it so completely that in the end,
to counterpoise my looking, an angel must come
as player and snatch up those stuffed bodies.
Angel and puppet: then finally there's a play.
Then comes together what we constantly
separate, simply by being here. Only then
emerges from our seasons the cycle
of the whole transformation. Then, above us and beyond,
the angel is playing.   See, the dying,
wouldn't they suspect how full of pretext
is everything that we achieve here. Nothing is
what it is. O hours of childhood,
when behind the figures there was more than just
things past, and the future not before us.
We grew, of course, and sometimes we hurried
to be grown up quickly, half for the sake of those
who had nothing left but being grown up.
And yet, in going on our own, we were
happy with what was permanent, and we stood there
in the in-between space between world and plaything,
at a place which from the beginning
had been founded for a pure event.

Who shows a child just as he stands? Who places

33

es ins Gestirn und gibt das Maß des Abstands
ihm in die Hand? Wer macht den Kindertod
aus grauem Brot, das hart wird, — oder läßt
ihn drin im runden Mund, so wie den Gröps   80
von einem schönen Apfel? . . . . . . Mörder sind
leicht einzusehen. Aber dies: den Tod,
den ganzen Tod, noch *vor* dem Leben so
sanft zu enthalten und nicht bös zu sein,
ist unbeschreiblich.   85

him in the constellation and puts the measuring rod of distance
into his hand? Who makes a child's death
out of gray bread that hardens, — or leaves
it inside his round mouth like the core
of a beautiful apple? . . . . . . Murderers are
easy to see through. But this: to contain death,
the whole of death, even *before* life, so
gently, and not be angry,
is indescribable.

Die Fünfte Elegie

Frau Hertha Koenig zugeeignet

Wer aber *sind* sie, sag mir, die Fahrenden, diese ein wenig
Flüchtigern noch als wir selbst, die dringend von früh an
wringt ein *wem, wem* zu Liebe
niemals zufriedener Wille? Sondern er wringt sie,
biegt sie, schlingt sie und schwingt sie,   5
wirft sie und fängt sie zurück; wie aus geölter,
glatterer Luft kommen sie nieder
auf dem verzehrten, von ihrem ewigen
Aufsprung dünneren Teppich, diesem verlorenen
Teppich im Weltall.   10
Aufgelegt wie ein Pflaster, als hätte der Vorstadt-
Himmel der Erde dort wehe getan.

                           Und kaum dort,
aufrecht, da und gezeigt: des Dastehns
großer Anfangsbuchstab . . . , schon auch, die stärksten   15
Männer, rollt sie wieder, zum Scherz, der immer
kommende Griff, wie August der Starke bei Tisch
einen zinnenen Teller.

Ach und um diese
Mitte, die Rose des Zuschauns: 20
blüht und entblättert. Um diesen
Stampfer, den Stempel, den von dem eignen

36

The Fifth Elegy

Dedicated to Mrs. Hertha Koenig

But who *are* they, tell me, the travelers, these even a little
more fleeting than we ourselves. A never satisfied will,
urgently pressing from early on, wrings them —
for *whose, whose* sake? Yet it wrings them,
bends them, loops them and swings them,
hurls them and catches them back; as though out of oiled
smoother air they come down
on the consumed carpet, made thin
by their eternal leaping, this lost
carpet in the cosmos.
Laid on like a bandage as if the suburb-
heavens had hurt the earth there.
                              And scarcely there,
upright, here and displayed: the large first letter
of *Dastehen* — "standing here". . . , already the strongest
men are rolled again, for fun, by the ever-
approaching grip, like Augustus the Strong at dinner rolling
a pewter plate.

Ah, and around this
center, the rose of onlooking:
blossoms and sheds its petals. Around this
pestle, the pistil, struck by the pollen of its own

blühenden Staub getroffnen, zur Scheinfrucht
wieder der Unlust befruchteten, ihrer
niemals bewußten, — glänzend mit dünnster 25
Oberfläche leicht scheinlächelnden Unlust.

   Da: der welke, faltige Stemmer,
der alte, der nur noch trommelt,
eingegangen in seiner gewaltigen Haut, als hätte sie früher
zwei Männer enthalten, und einer 30
läge nun schon auf dem Kirchhof, und er überlebte den andern,
taub und manchmal ein wenig
wirr, in der verwitweten Haut.

Aber der junge, der Mann, als wär er der Sohn eines Nackens
und einer Nonne: prall und strammig erfüllt 35
mit Muskeln und Einfalt.

Oh ihr,
die ein Leid, das noch klein war,
einst als Spielzeug bekam, in einer seiner
langen Genesungen 40

Du, der mit dem Aufschlag,
wie nur Früchte ihn kennen, unreif,
täglich hundertmal abfällt vom Baum der gemeinsam
erbauten Bewegung, (der, rascher als Wasser, in wenig
Minuten Lenz, Sommere und Herbst hat) — 45

38

blossom, inseminating reluctance again
to become fake fruit, — never conscious
of the glittering thinnest veneer
of their light fake-smiling reluctance.

   Here: the sagging, wrinkled weight-lifter,
the old one, who only drums now,
shrunk in his mighty skin as if it once
contained *two* men and one now
lay in the churchyard, and he outlived the other,
deaf and sometimes a little
confused in his widowed skin.

But the young one, the man, as though the son of a neck
and a nun: stuffed tight and bulging
with muscles and mindlessness.

Oh you,
whom a sorrow, that was still small,
once received as a plaything, in one of its
long convalescences . . . .

You, who with the impact
known only to fruit, unripe,
fall a hundred times a day from the tree of mutually
built movement (which quicker than water, in a few
minutes has spring, summer, and autumn) —

abfällt und anprallt ans Grab:
manchmal, in halber Pause, will dir ein liebes
Antlitz entstehn hinüber zu deiner selten
zärtlichen Mutter; doch an deinen Körper verliert sich,
der es flächig verbraucht, das schüchtern   50
kaum versuchte Gesicht . . . Und wieder
klatscht der Mann in die Hand zu dem Ansprung, und eh dir
jemals ein Schmerz deutlicher wird in der Nähe des immer
trabenden Herzens, kommt das Brennen der Fußsohln
ihm, seinem Ursprung, zuvor mit ein paar dir   55
rasch in die Augen gejagten leiblichen Tränen.
Und dennoch, blindlings,
das Lächeln . . . . .

Engel! o nimms, pflücks, das kleinblütige Heilkraut.
Schaff eine Vase, verwahrs! Stells unter jene, uns *noch* nicht   60
offenen Freuden; in lieblicher Urne
rühms mit blumiger schwungiger Aufschrift:
                                        >*Subrisio Saltat.*<.

Du dann, Liebliche,
du, von den reizendsten Freuden   65
stumm Übersprungne. Vielleicht sind
deine Fransen glücklich für dich —,
oder über den jungen
prallen Brüsten die grüne metallene Seide
fühlt sich unendlich verwöhnt und entbehrt nichts.   70

40

fall off and crash against the grave:
sometimes, in a half-pause, a loving
look wants to emerge toward your seldom
tender mother; but that shy,
scarcely attempted face gets lost,
used up on your body's surface . . . And again
the man claps his hands for another leap, and always,
before a pain can get clearer near your ever-
trotting heart, the burning of your soles
anticipates it, its origin, with a few bodily tears
quickly chased into your eyes.
And nevertheless, blindly,
the smile . . . . .

Angel! o, take it, pluck it, the small-flowered healing herb.
Fetch a vase, keep it safe! Set it among those joys
not *yet* open to us; in a lovely urn
praise it with flowery flourished inscription:

>*Subrisio Saltat.*<.

You then, lovely one,
you, silently passed over
by the most delightful of joys. Perhaps
your fringes are happy for you —,
or over your young
firm breasts the green metallic silk
feels infinitely indulged and lacks nothing.

Du,
immerfort anders auf alle des Gleichgewichts schwankende Waagen
hingelegte Marktfrucht des Gleichmuts,
öffentlich unter den Schultern.

Wo, o *wo* ist der Ort — ich trag ihn im Herzen —,   75
wo sie noch lange nich *konnten*, noch von einander
abfiln, wie sich bespringende, nicht recht
paarige Tiere; —
wo die Gewichte noch schwer sind;
wo noch von ihren vergeblich   80
wirbelnden Stäben die Teller
torkeln . . . . .

Und plötzlich in diesem mühsamen Nirgends, plötzlich
die unsägliche Stelle, wo sich das reine Zuwenig
unbegreiflich verwandelt —, umspringt   85
in jenes leere Zuviel.
Wo die vielstellige Rechnung
zahlenlos aufgeht.

Plätze, o Platz in Paris, unendlicher Schauplatz,
wo die Modistin, *Madame Lamort*,   90
die ruhlosen Wege der Erde, endlose Bänder,
schlingt und windet und neue aus ihnen
Schleifen erfindet, Rüschen, Blumen, Kokarden, künstliche Früchte —,
unwahr gefärbt, — für die billigen   alle

42

You,
market fruit of equanimity, laid out in constant variety
on all the balanced, swaying scales,
public below the shoulders.

Where, o *where* is the place — I carry it in my heart —,
where they *could* not *do* it yet, still fell away
from each other like mounting animals
not suitably paired; —
where the weights are still heavy;
where still, from their vainly
twirling sticks, the plates
reel . . . . .

And suddenly in this toilsome nowhere, suddenly
the inexpressible point where the pure too little
incomprehensibly transforms itself —, suddenly shifts
into that empty too much.
Where the many-numbered computation
comes out even.

Squares, o square in Paris, unending showplace,
where the milliner, *Madame Lamort,*
loops and winds the restless paths of the earth,
endless ribbons, and fashions from them
new bows, frills, flowers, cockades, artificial fruit —, all
falsely colored, — for the cheap

Winterhüte des Schicksals.

. . . .

Engel!: Es wäre ein Platz, den wir nicht wissen, und dorten,
auf unsäglichem Teppich, zeigten die Liebenden, die's hier
bis zum Können nie bringen, ihre kühnen
hohen Figuren des Herzschwungs,
ihre Türme aus Lust, ihre   100
längst, wo Boden nie war, nur an einander
lehnenden Leitern, bebend, — und *könntens*,
vor den Zuschauern rings, unzähligen lautlosen Toten:
    Würfen die dann ihre letzten, immer ersparten,
immer verborgenen, die wir nicht kennen, ewig   105
gültigen Münzen des Glücks vor das endlich
wahrhaft lächelnde Paar auf gestilltem
Teppich?

winter hats of fate.

. . . .

Angel!: would there be a place we don't know, and there
on an indescribable carpet the lovers, who here
are never able to do it, would show their daring
high figures of the heartswing,
their towers of pleasure, their
ladders, where ground never was, leaning long since
just on each other, trembling — and *could do it,*
before the surrounding spectators, the countless soundless dead:

    Would they then fling their last, always saved up,
always hidden, unknown to us, eternally
valid coins of happiness before the finally
genuinely smiling pair on the quieted
carpet?

Die Sechste Elegie

Feigenbaum, seit wie lange schon ists mir bedeutend,
wie du die Blüte beinah ganz überschlägst
und hinein in die zeitig entschlossene Frucht,
ungerühmt, drängst dein reines Geheimnis.
Wie der Fontäne Rohr treibt dein gebognes Gezweig   5
abwärts den Saft und hinan: und er springt aus dem Schlaf,
fast nicht erwachend, ins Glück seiner süßesten Leistung.
Sieh: wie der Gott in den Schwan.

      . . . . . . Wir aber verweilen,
ach, uns rühmt es zu blühn, und ins verspätete Innre   10
unserer endlichen Frucht gehn wir verraten hinein.
Wenigen steigt so stark der Andrang des Handelns,
daß sie schon anstehn und glühn in der Fülle des Herzens,
wenn die Verführung zum Blühn wie gelinderte Nachtluft
ihnen die Jugend des Munds, ihnen die Lider berührt: 15
Helden vielleicht und den frühe Hinüberbestimmten,
denen der gärtnernde Tod anders die Adern verbiegt.
Diese stürzen dahin: dem eigenen Lächeln
sind sie voran, wie das Rossegespann in den milden
muldigen Bildern von Karnak dem siegenden König.   20

Wunderlich nah ist der Held doch den jugendlich Toten. Dauern
ficht ihn nicht an. Sein Aufgang ist Dasein; beständig
nimmt er sich fort und tritt ins veränderte Sternbild
seiner steten Gefahr. Dort fänden ihn wenige. Aber,

46

The Sixth Elegy

Fig tree, for how long now has it been meaningful to me
the way you almost completely bypass flowering
and into the early-determined fruit,
unpraised, urge your pure secret.
Like the fountain's pipe your curved branches drive
the sap downward and up: and it springs from sleep,
almost without awakening, into the joy of its sweetest achievement.
See: like the god into the swan.
      . . . . . . But we linger,
ah, our pride is in blossoming, and we enter
the delayed interior of our final fruit betrayed.
For few the urge to action rises so strongly that they stand
waiting already, glowing in the fullness of their hearts
when the temptation to blossom touches, like softened night air,
the youth of their lips, their eyelids:
heroes perhaps, and those fated for an early crossing,
whose veins gardening death has twisted differently.
These plunge on: they're ahead of
their own smile, like the team of horses in the gentle
bas-reliefs of the victorious king at Karnak.

Strangely similar to the young dead is the hero. Lasting
doesn't concern him. Being is his ascent; steadily
he impels himself onward and steps into the altered constellation
of his constant danger. There few would find him. But

47

das uns finster verschweigt, das plötzlich begeisterte Schicksal 25
singt ihn hinein in den Sturm seiner aufrauschenden Welt.
Hör ich doch keinen wie *ihn*. Auf einmal durchgeht mich
mit der strömenden Luft sein verdunkelter Ton.

Dann, wie verbärg ich mich gern vor der Sehnsucht: O wär ich,
wär ich ein Knabe und dürft es noch werden und säße 30
in die künftigen Arme gestützt und läse von Simson,
wie seine Mutter erst nichts und dann alles gebar.

War er nicht Held schon in dir, o Mutter, begann nicht
dort schon, in dir, seine herrische Auswahl?
Tausende brauten im Schooß und wollten *er* sein, 35
aber sieh: er ergriff und ließ aus —, wählte und konnte.
Und wenn er Säulen zerstieß, so wars, da er ausbrach
aus der Welt deines Leibs in die engere Welt, wo er weiter
wählte und konnte. O Mütter der Helden, o Ursprung
reißender Ströme! Ihr Schluchten, in die sich 40
hoch von dem Herzrand, klagend,
schon die Mädchen gestürzt, künftig die Opfer dem Sohn.

Denn hinstürmte der Held durch Aufenthalte der Liebe,
jeder hob ihn hinaus, jeder ihn meinende Herzschlag,
abgewendet schon, stand er am Ende der Lächeln, anders. 45

darkly silencing us, a suddenly-impassioned destiny
sings him into the storm, the surging roar of his world.
I hear no one like *him*. Suddenly, his darkened tone goes
through me with the streaming air.

Then, how gladly I would hide from the yearning: oh were I,
were I a boy and might still become one, and could sit
supported in the future arms, and could read of Samson,
how his mother gave birth at first to nothing and then to everything.

Was he not a hero already inside you, oh mother, did not
his lordly choosing already begin there, inside you?
Thousands were brewing in the womb and wanted to be *him*,
but look: he seized and omitted—, chose and succeeded.
And if he crushed pillars, it was when he broke out
of the world of your body into the narrower world where he still
chose and prevailed. Oh mothers of heroes, oh spring
of tearing streams! You ravines into which,
high from the edge of the heart, wailing,
girls have already hurled themselves, future sacrifices to the son.

For the hero stormed on through sojourns of love,
each lifted him up and away, each heartbeat meant for him;
already turned beyond, he stood at the end of all smiles, changed.

Die Siebente Elegie

Werbung nicht mehr, nicht Werbung, entwachsene Stimme,
sei deines Schreies Natur; zwar schrieest du rein wie der Vogel,
wenn ihn die Jahreszeit aufhebt, die steigende, beinah vergessend,
daß er ein kümmerndes Tier und nicht nur ein einzelnes Herz sei,
das sie ins Heitere wirft, in die innigen Himmel. Wie er, so   5
würbest du wohl, nicht minder —, daß, noch unsichtbar,
dich die Freundin erführ, die stille, in der eine Antwort
langsam erwacht und über dem Hören sich anwärmt, —
deinem erkühnten Gefühl die erglühte Gefühlin.

O und der Frühling begriffe —, da ist keine Stelle,   10
die nicht trüge den Ton der Verkündigung. Erst jenen kleinen
fragenden Auflaut, den mit steigernder Stille,
weithin umschweigt ein reiner bejahender Tag.
Dann die Stufen hinan, Ruf-Stufen hinan, zum geträumten
Tempel der Zukunft —; dann den Triller, Fontäne,   15
die zu dem drängenden Strahl schon das Fallen zuvornimmt
im versprechlichen Spiel . . . Und vor sich, den Sommer.

Nicht nur die Morgen alle des Sommers —, nicht nur
wie sie sich wandeln in Tag und strahlen vor Anfang.
Nicht nur die Tage, die zart sind um Blumen, und oben,   20
um die gestalteten Bäume, stark und gewaltig.
Nicht nur die Andacht dieser entfalteten Kräfte,
nicht nur die Wege, nicht nur die Wiesen im Abend,

50

The Seventh Elegy

Wooing no more, not wooing, outgrown voice,
be the nature of your cry; although you cried purely like the bird
when the season — the ascending one — lifts him up, almost forgetting
that he's a troubled animal and not just a single heart
flung into brightness, into the tender skies. Like him,
you, still unseen, would woo well, no less well —, so that
the beloved, the silent one, would begin to know you, in her an answer
slowly awakens and grows warm with hearing —
toward your emboldened feeling her ignited feeling.

Oh and the springtime would grasp it —, there's no place
that wouldn't carry the sound of annunciation. First that small
questioning note which a pure affirming day, with
growing stillness far and wide, surrounds with silence.
Then up the steps, up the call-steps to the dreamed-of
temple of the future —; then the trill, fountain
whose jet-thrust already anticipates,
in promising play, its falling . . . And ahead, the summer.

Not only all the mornings of summer —, not only
the way they change into day and radiate with beginning.
Not only the days, that are gentle around flowers, and above,
around the formed trees, mighty and powerful.
Not only the reverence of these unfurled forces,
not only the paths, not only the meadows in the evening,

nicht nur, nach spätem Gewitter, das atmende Klarsein,
nicht nur der nahende Schlaf und ein Ahnen, abends . . . 25
sondern die Nächte! Sondern die hohen, des Sommers,
Nächte, sondern die Sterne, die Sterne der Erde.
O einst tot sein und sie wissen unendlich,
alle die Sterne: denn wie, wie, wie sie vergessen!

Siehe, da rief ich die Liebende. Aber nicht *sie* nur 30
käme . . . Es kämen aus schwächlichen Gräbern
Mädchen und ständen . . . Denn, wie beschränk ich,
wie, den gerufenen Ruf? Die Versunkenen suchen
immer noch Erde. — Ihr Kinder, ein hiesig
einmal ergriffenes Ding gälte für viele. 35
Glaubt nicht, Schicksal sei mehr, als das Dichte der Kindheit;
wie überholtet ihr oft den Geliebten, atmend,
atmend nach seligem Lauf, auf nichts zu, ins Freie.

Hiersein ist herrlich. Ihr wußtet es, Mädchen, *ihr* auch,
die ihr scheinbar entbehrtet, versank —, ihr, in den ärgsten 40
Gassen der Städte, Schwärende, oder dem Abfall
Offene. Denn eine Stunde war jeder, vielleicht nicht
ganz eine Stunde, ein mit den Maßen der Zeit kaum
Meßliches zwischen zwei Weilen —, da sie ein Dasein
hatte. Alles. Die Adern voll Dasein. 45
Nur, wir vergessen so leicht, was der lachende Nachbar
uns nicht bestätigt oder beneidet. Sichtbar
wollen wirs heben, wo doch das sichtbarste Glück uns

not only, after a late storm, the breathing clarity,
not only approaching sleep and a premonition, in the evenings . . .
but the nights! But the summer's high nights,
but the stars, the stars of the earth.
Oh to have been dead and know them infinitely,
all the stars: for how, how, how to forget them!

See, I have called the beloved. But not *she* alone
would come . . . Out of frail graves would come
young girls, and stand . . . For how do I limit,
how, the called-out call? The sunken ones are still searching
for the earth. — You children, a thing
of our world grasped once would count for many.
Do not believe that destiny is more than the density of childhood;
how often you overtook the beloved, breathing,
breathing after blissful running, towards nothing, into the Open.

Being here is magnificent. You knew it, girls, even *you*,
who seemed so deprived, sunk so low —, you, in the most
wretched streets of the cities, festering, or open for
offal. For each one was given an hour, perhaps not
a whole hour, an instant between two moments
scarcely measurable as time —, when she had
her being. Everything. Her veins full of being.
But we forget so easily what our laughing neighbor
doesn't confirm for us, nor envy. We want to lift it
into visibility, when the most visible happiness

53

erst zu erkennen sich gibt, wenn wir es innen verwandeln.

Nirgends, Geliebte, wird Welt sein, als innen. Unser   50
Leben geht hin mit Verwandlung. Und immer geringer
schwindet das Außen. Wo einmal ein dauerndes Haus war,
schlägt sich erdachtes Gebild vor, quer, zu Erdenklichem
völlig gehörig, als ständ es noch ganz im Gehirne.
Weite Speicher der Kraft schafft sich der Zeitgeist, gestaltlos   55
wie der spannende Drang, den er aus allem gewinnt.
Tempel kennt er nicht mehr. Diese, des Herzens, Verschwendung
sparen wir heimlicher ein. Ja, wo noch eins übersteht,
ein einst gebetetes Ding, ein gedientes, gekniees —,
hält es sich, so wie es ist, schon ins Unsichtbare hin.   60
Viele gewahrens nicht mehr, doch ohne den Vorteil,
daß sie's nun *innerlich* baun, mit Pfeilern und Statuen, größer!

Jede dumpfe Umkehr der Welt hat solche Enterbte,
denen das Frühere nicht und noch nicht das Nächste gehört.
Denn auch das Nächste ist weit für die Menschen. *Uns* soll   65
dies nicht verwirren; es stärke in uns die Bewahrung
der noch erkannten Gestalt. — Dies *stand* einmal unter Menschen,
mitten im Schicksal stands, im vernichtenden, mitten
im Nichtwissen-Wohin stand es, wie seiend, und bog
Sterne zu sich aus gesicherten Himmeln. Engel,   70
dir noch zeig ich es, *da*! in deinem Anschaun
steh es gerettet zuletzt, nun endlich aufrecht.
Säulen, Pylone, der Sphinx, das strebende Stemmen,

54

reveals itself to us only when we transform it within.

Nowhere, beloved, will world be but within. Our
life goes by in transformations. And ever-shrinking,
the external vanishes. Where once there was an enduring house,
a cerebral creation offers itself, athwart, belonging
fully to the conceivable, as though it still stood entirely in the brain.
The spirit of our age builds itself vast stores of power, formless
as the tensed driving force it wrests from all things.
It no longer recognizes temples. These, an extravagance of the heart,
we save up more secretly. Yes, where there still survives
a thing once prayed to, served, knelt to —,
it already takes itself, just as it is, into the invisible.
Many are no longer aware of that, though without the benefit
of building it now *inwardly*, with pillars and statues, greater!

Each dull, heavy turn of the world has such disinherited ones
who possess neither what is past nor what is to come.
For even what's next is far off for a human being. This shouldn't
bewilder *us*; may it strengthen in us the safekeeping of
the still-recognized form. — This *stood* once among mankind,
it stood in the midst of destiny, the annihilating one, in the midst of
not-knowing-where-to it stood, as if it existed, and bent
stars to itself from fortified heavens. Angel,
to *you* I will show it, *there*! in your gaze
let it stand rescued at last, now finally upright.
Columns, pylons, the Sphinx, the striving tension

grau aus vergehender Stadt oder aus fremder, des Doms.

War es nicht Wunder? O staune, Engel, denn *wir* sinds,   75
wir, o du Großer, erzähls, daß wir solches vermochten, mein Atem
reicht für die Rühmung nicht aus. So haben wir dennoch
nicht die Räume versäumt, diese gewährenden, diese
unseren Räume. (Was müssen sie fürchterlich groß sein,
da sie Jahrtausende nicht unseres Fühlns überfülln.)   80
Aber ein Turm war groß, nicht wahr? O Engel, er war es, —
groß, auch noch neben dir? Chartres war groß —, und Musik
reichte noch weiter hinan und überstieg uns. Doch selbst nur
eine Liebende —, oh, allein am nächtlichen Fenster . . . ,
reichte sie dir nicht ans Knie —?   85
                    Glaub *nicht*, daß ich werbe.
Engel, und würb ich dich auch! Du kommst nicht. Denn mein
Anruf ist immer voll Hinweg; wider so starke
Strömung kannst du nicht schreiten. Wie ein gestreckter
Arm ist mein Rufen. Und seine zum Greifen   90
oben offene Hand bleibt vor dir
offen, wie Abwehr und Warnung,
Unfaßlicher, weitauf.

of the cathedral, gray from a fading or an alien city.

Was it not a miracle? Oh stand amazed, angel, for *we* are the ones,
we, oh you great one, proclaim it, that we could do such things,
I don't have breath enough for such praise. So after all we've
not neglected the spaces, these giving, these
our spaces. (How frightfully great they must be,
since thousands of years of our feelings don't overflow them.)
But a tower was great, was it not? Oh, angel, so it was, —
great, even next to you? Chartres was great —, and music
reached even higher and rose beyond us. But even
just one woman in love —, oh, alone at the window by night . . . ,
did she not come up to your knee —?

                       Don't think I'm wooing.
Angel, and even if I were to woo you! You don't come. For my
call to you is always full of Away; against so strong
a current you cannot stride. Like an outstretched
arm is my call. And its hand, lifted up and
open, ready to seize you, stays open before you,
like rejection and warning,
ungraspable one, far above.

Die Achte Elegie

Rudolf Kassner zugeeignet

Mit allen Augen sieht die Kreatur
das Offene. Nur unsre Augen sind
wie umgekehrt und ganz um sie gestellt
als Fallen, rings um ihren freien Ausgang.
Was draußen *ist*, wir wissens aus des Tiers   5
Antlitz allein; denn schon das frühe Kind
wenden wir um und zwingens, daß es rückwärts
Gestaltung sehe, nicht das Offne, das
im Tiergesicht so tief ist. Frei von Tod.
Ihn sehen wir allein; das freie Tier   10
hat seinen Untergang stets hinter sich
und vor sich Gott, und wenn es geht, so gehts
in Ewigkeit, so wie die Brunnen gehen.
      Wir haben nie, nicht einen einzigen Tag,
den reinen Raum vor uns, in den die Blumen   15
unendlich aufgehn. Immer ist es Welt
und niemals Nirgends ohne Nicht: das Reine,
Unüberwachte, das man atmet und
unendlich *weiß* und nicht begehrt. Als Kind
verliert sich eins im Stilln an dies und wird   20
gerüttelt. Oder jener stirbt und *ists*.
Denn nah am Tod sieht man den Tod nicht mehr
und starrt *hinaus*, vielleicht mit großem Tierblick.

58

The Eighth Elegy

dedicated to Rudolf Kassner

With all its eyes the creature sees
the Open. Only our eyes are
as though reversed, and placed all around them
as traps, encircling their free exit.
What *is* outside we only know from the animal's
countenance; for already we turn around
the young child and force it to see backwards,
see form, not the Open that's
so deep in the animal face. Free of death—
it, only we see. The free animal
has its demise always behind it
and before it God, and when it moves, it moves
in eternity, as the fountains move.

We never have, not for a single day,
the pure space before us into which the flowers
endlessly unfold. Always it is world
and never Nowhere without Not: the pure,
the unwatched, that one breathes and
infinitely *knows* and does not covet. As a child
one gets lost there in the silence and is
shaken back. Or someone dies and so *becomes it*.
For near to death, one sees death no longer
and stares *out*, perhaps with the wide animal gaze.

Liebende, wäre nicht der andre, der
die Sicht verstellt, sind nah daran und staunen . . .   25
Wie aus Versehn ist ihnen aufgetan
hinter dem andern . . . Aber über ihn
kommt keiner fort, und wieder wird ihm Welt.
Der Schöpfung immer zugewendet, sehn
wir nur auf ihr die Spiegelung des Frein,   30
von uns verdunkelt. Oder daß ein Tier,
ein stummes, aufschaut, ruhig durch uns durch.
Dieses heißt Schicksal: gegenüber sein
und nichts als das und immer gegenüber.

Wäre Bewußtheit unsrer Art in dem   35
sicheren Tier, das uns entgegenzieht
in anderer Richtung —, riß es uns herum
mit seinem Wandel. Doch sein Sein ist ihm
unendlich, ungefaßt und ohne Blick
auf seinen Zustand, rein, so wie sein Ausblick.   40
Und wo wir Zukunft sehn, dort sieht es Alles
und sich in Allem und geheilt für immer.

Und doch ist in dem wachsam warmen Tier
Gewicht und Sorge einer großen Schwermut.
Denn ihm auch haftet immer an, was uns   45
oft überwältigt, — die Erinnerung,
als sei schon einmal das, wonach man drängt,
näher gewesen, treuer und sein Anschluß

60

Lovers, were it not for the other, who
blocks the view, are close to it, and marvel . . .
As if by mistake, it opens up to them
behind the other . . . But no one
gets beyond, and again it's world for him.
Turned always to the created, we see
in it only the reflection of the free,
darkened by us. Or that an animal,
wordless, looks up, calmly, through and through us.
This is called destiny: to be opposite
and nothing but that and always opposite.

Were consciousness of our kind in the
sure animal that moves toward us
in the other direction —, it would spin us around
with its transformation. But to it, its being is
unending, ungrasped and without a glance
at its condition, pure, like its outward gaze.
And where we see the future, there it sees All
and itself in All and healed forever.

And yet, within the warm watchful animal, there is
the weight and care of a great sadness.
For to it also always clings what
often overwhelms us, — the memory,
as if what we struggle toward
had once been nearer, truer, and its bond

unendlich zärtlich. Hier ist alles Abstand,
und dort wars Atem. Nach der ersten Heimat   50
ist ihm die zweite zwitterig und windig.
  O Seligkeit der *kleinen* Kreatur,
die immer *bleibt* im Schooße, der sie austrug;
o Glück der Mücke, die noch *innen* hüpft,
selbst wenn sie Hochzeit hat: denn Schooß ist Alles.   55
Und sieh die halbe Sicherheit des Vogels,
der beinah beides weiß aus seinem Ursprung,
als wär er eine Seele der Etrusker,
aus einem Toten, den ein Raum empfing,
doch mit der ruhenden Figur als Deckel.   60
Und wie bestürzt ist eins, das fliegen muß
und stammt aus einem Schooß. Wie vor sich selbst
erschreckt, durchzuckts die Luft, wie wenn ein Sprung
durch eine Tasse geht. So reißt die Spur
der Fledermaus durchs Porzellan des Abends.   65

Und wir: Zuschauer, immer, überall,
dem allen zugewandt und nie hinaus!
Uns überfüllts. Wir ordnens. Es zerfällt.
Wir ordnens wieder und zerfallen selbst.

Wer hat uns also umgedreht, daß wir,   70
was wir auch tun, in jener Haltung sind
von einem, welcher fortgeht? Wie er auf

infinitely tender. Here all is distance
and there it was breath. After the first home
the second one feels ambiguous and windy.
   Oh bliss of the *tiny* creature,
who forever *stays* in the womb that bore it;
oh luck of the gnat, which still skips about *inside,*
even on its wedding day: for womb is All.
And see the half-certainty of the bird
who from its very origin almost knows both,
as though it were a soul of the Etruscans,
from one of their dead, welcomed by a space
but with the resting figure as a lid.
And how dismayed is one who has to fly
and yet springs from a womb. As if startled
by itself, it flashes through the air like a crack
going through a cup. So the track of the bat
rips through the porcelain of the evening.

And we: spectators, always, everywhere,
turned toward all that and never outward!
It fills us to overflowing. We order it. It falls apart.
We order it again and fall apart ourselves.

Who has so turned us around that we,
whatever we do, are in that posture
of someone who is leaving? Like him who, on

dem letzten Hügel, der ihm ganz sein Tal
noch einmal zeigt, sich wendet, anhält, weilt —,
so leben wir und nehmen immer Abschied.

75

the last hill, which shows him his whole valley
one more time, turns, stops, lingers —,
so do we live and forever take our leave.

Die Neunte Elegie

Warum, wenn es angeht, also die Frist des Daseins
hinzubringen, als Lorbeer, ein wenig dunkler als alles
andere Grün, mit kleinen Wellen an jedem
Blattrand (wie eines Windes Lächeln) —: warum dann
Menschliches müssen — und, Schicksal vermeidend,   5
sich sehnen nach Schicksal? . . .

                              Oh, *nicht*, weil Glück *ist*,
dieser voreilige Vorteil eines nahen Verlusts.
Nicht aus Neugier, oder zur Übung des Herzens,
das auch im Lorbeer *wäre*   10

Aber weil Hiersein viel ist, und weil uns scheinbar
alles das Hiesige braucht, dieses Schwindende, das
seltsam uns angeht. Uns, die Schwindendsten. *Ein* Mal
jedes, nur *ein* Mal. *Ein* Mal und nichtmehr. Und wir auch
ein Mal. Nie wieder. Aber dieses   15
ein Mal gewesen zu sein, wenn auch nur *ein* Mal:
irdisch gewesen zu sein, scheint nicht widerrufbar.

Und so drängen wir uns und wollen es leisten,
wollens enthalten in unsern einfachen Händen,
im überfüllteren Blick und im sprachlosen Herzen.   20
Wollen es werden. — Wem es geben? Am liebsten
alles behalten für immer . . . Ach, in den andern Bezug,

The Ninth Elegy

Why, when we could spend our time of being
as laurel, a little darker than all
other green, with little waves on each
leaf edge (like a wind's smile) —: why then
the compulsion to do what is human — and, evading destiny,
long for destiny? . . .

                       Oh *not* because happiness *is*,
this hasty profit from an impending loss.
Not from curiosity, or for practice of the heart,
which in the laurel too *would be* . . . . .

But because being here is much, and because apparently
all that's here needs us, this fleeting world that
strangely entreats us. Us, the most fleeting. *One* time
each, only *one* time. *One* time and no more. And we also
one time. Never again. But to have been,
this *one* time, even if only *one* time:
to have been *earthly*, seems beyond recall.

And so we press on and want to achieve it,
want to contain it in our simple hands,
in our overcrowded eyes and in our speechless heart.
Want to become it. — Give it to whom? Best of all
to keep everything forever . . . Ah, into the other realm,

wehe, was nimmt man hinüber? Nicht das Anschaun, das hier
langsam erlernte, und kein hier Ereignetes. Keins.
Also die Schmerzen. Also vor allem das Schwersein,   25
also der Liebe lange Erfahrung, — also
lauter Unsägliches. Aber später,
unter den Sternen, was solls: *die* sind *besser* unsäglich.
Bringt doch der Wanderer auch vom Hange des Bergrands
nicht eine Hand voll Erde ins Tal, die Allen unsägliche, sondern   30
ein erworbenes Wort, reines, den gelben und blaun
Enzian. Sind wir vielleicht *hier*, um zu sagen: Haus,
Brücke, Brunnen, Tor, Krug, Obstbaum, Fenster, —
höchstens: Säule, Turm . . . . . aber zu *sagen*, verstehs,
oh zu sagen *so*, wie selber die Dinge niemals   35
innig meinten zu sein. Ist nicht die heimliche List
dieser verschwiegenen Erde, wenn sie die Liebenden drängt,
daß sich in ihrem Gefühl jedes und jedes entzückt?
Schwelle: was ists für zwei
Liebende, daß sie die eigne ältere Schwelle der Tür   40
ein wenig verbrauchen, auch sie, nach den vielen vorher
und vor den Künftigen . . . . , leicht.

Hier ist des *Säglichen* Zeit, *hier* seine Heimat.
Sprich und bekenn. Mehr als je
fallen die Dinge dahin, die erlebbaren, denn,   45
was sie verdrängend ersetzt, ist ein Tun ohne Bild.
Tun unter Krusten, die willig zerspringen, sobald
innen das Handeln entwächst und sich anders begrenzt.

alas, what does one take across? Not our discernment, learned here
so slowly, and nothing that took place here. Nothing.
So the suffering. So above all what's difficult,
so the long experience of love, — so
all that's beyond words. But later,
among the stars, what good is it: *they* are *better* without words.
After all, the wanderer brings from the mountain slopes
into the valley not a hand full of earth, inexpressible to all, but
an acquired word, pure, the yellow and blue
gentian. Are we perhaps *here* in order to say: house,
bridge, fountain, gate, pitcher, fruit tree, window, —
at most: column, tower . . . . . but to *say*, understand it,
oh, to say them, as these things never
imagined themselves being so tender. Isn't it the secret cunning
of this concealing earth, when she urges the lovers on,
that each and every thing becomes enraptured in their feeling?
Threshold: what is it for two
lovers to use up their own door's ancient threshold
a little, they too, after the many before them
and before those still to come . . . . , lightly.

Here is the time of the *sayable, here* its homeland.
Speak and bear witness. More than ever
the things fall aside, the tangible things; for
what drives them out and takes their place is an act without image.
An act under crusts that willingly crack open as soon as
the action within outgrows them and sets other limits.

Zwischen den Hämmern besteht
unser Herz, wie die Zunge   50
zwischen den Zähnen, die doch,
dennoch, die preisende bleibt.

Preise dem Engel die Welt, nicht die unsägliche, *ihm*
kannst du nicht großtun mit herrlich Erfühltem; im Weltall,
wo er fühlender fühlt, bist du ein Neuling. Drum zeig   55
ihm das Einfache, das, von Geschlecht zu Geschlechtern gestaltet,
als ein Unsriges lebt, neben der Hand und im Blick.
Sag ihm die Dinge. Er wird staunender stehn; wie du standest
bei dem Seiler in Rom, oder beim Töpfer am Nil.
Zeig ihm, wie glücklich ein Ding sein kann, wie schuldlos und unser, 60
wie selbst das klagende Leid rein zur Gestalt sich entschließt,
dient als ein Ding, oder stirbt in ein Ding —, und jenseits
selig der Geige entgeht. — Und diese, von Hingang
lebenden Dinge verstehn, daß du sie rühmst; vergänglich,
traun sie ein Rettendes uns, den Vergänglichsten, zu.   65
Wollen, wir sollen sie ganz im unsichtbaren Herzen verwandeln
in — o, unendlich in uns! wer wir am Ende auch seien.

Erde, ist es nicht dies, was du willst: *unsichtbar*
in uns erstehn? — Ist es dein Traum nicht,
einmal unsichtbar zu sein? — Erde! unsichtbar!   70
Was, wenn Verwandlung nicht, ist dein drängender Auftrag?
Erde, du liebe, ich will. Oh glaub, es bedürfte
nicht deiner Frühlinge mehr, mich dir zu gewinnen —, *einer*,

Between the hammers endures
our heart, like the tongue
between the teeth, which yet,
nevertheless, goes on praising.

Praise the world to the angel, not the unsayable, to *him*
you cannot strut your magnificent feeling. In the universe,
where he more feelingly feels, you are a novice. Therefore, show
him the simplicity of things, which, formed from generation to
lives as one of us, near at hand and within sight.   [generation,
Tell him of the things. He will stand more astonished; as you stood
by the rope-maker in Rome or by the potter on the Nile.
Show him how happy a thing can be, how guiltless and ours,
how even lamenting grief purely commits to form,
serves as a thing or dies into a thing —, and beyond,
blissfully escapes the violin. — And these things,
which live by passing away, understand that you praise them; transient,
they trust us to rescue them — us, the most transient.
They want us to transform them utterly in our invisible hearts
— oh, unendingly into us! Whoever in the end we might be.

Earth, is it not this you want: to arise
invisible within us? — Is it not your dream
to be invisible some day? — Earth! invisible!
What, if not transformation, is your urgent mission?
Earth, you beloved, I will. Oh, believe me, it would not take
more of your springtimes to win me over —, *one,*

ach, ein einziger ist schon dem Blute zu viel.
Namenlos bin ich zu dir entschlossen, von weit her.   75
Immer warst du im Recht, und dein heiliger Einfall
ist der vertrauliche Tod.

Siehe, ich lebe. Woraus? Weder Kindheit noch Zukunft
werden weniger . . . . . Überzähliges Dasein
entspringt mir im Herzen.   80

ah, just one is already too much for my blood.
I'm utterly committed to you, from long ago.
You were always right, and your holy inspiration
is our intimate Death.

Look, I live. From what? Neither childhood nor future
diminishes . . . . . Immeasurable being
springs up in my heart.

Die Zehnte Elegie

Daß ich dereinst, an dem Ausgang der grimmigen Einsicht,
Jubel und Ruhm aufsinge zustimmenden Engeln.
Daß von den klar geschlagenen Hämmern des Herzens
keiner versage an weichen, zweifelnden oder
reißenden Saiten. Daß mich mein strömendes Antlitz   5
glänzender mache; daß das unscheinbare Weinen
blühe. O wie werdet ihr dann, Nächte, mir lieb sein,
gehärmte. Daß ich euch knieender nicht, untröstliche Schwestern,
hinnahm, nicht in euer gelöstes
Haar mich gelöster ergab. Wir, Vergeuder der Schmerzen.   10
Wie wir sie absehn voraus, in die traurige Dauer,
ob sie nicht enden vielleicht. Sie aber sind ja
unser winterwähriges Laub, unser dunkeles Sinngrün,
eine der Zeiten des heimlichen Jahres —, nicht nur
Zeit —, sind Stelle, Siedelung, Lager, Boden, Wohnort.   15

Freilich, wehe, wie fremd sind die Gassen der Leid-Stadt,
wo in der falschen, aus Übertönung gemachten
Stille, stark, aus der Gußform des Leeren der Ausguß,
prahlt: der vergoldete Lärm, das platzende Denkmal.
O, wie spurlos zerträte ein Engel ihnen den Trostmarkt,   20
den die Kirche begrenzt, ihre fertig gekaufte:
reinlich und zu und enttäuscht wie ein Postamt am Sonntag.
Draußen aber kräuseln sich immer die Ränder von Jahrmarkt.
Schaukeln der Freiheit! Taucher und Gaukler des Eifers!

The Tenth Elegy

Oh that one day, at the end of this grim insight, I
may sing out jubilation and praise to assenting angels.
That of the clear-struck hammers of my heart
not one fail because of slack, doubting or
breaking strings. That my streaming face
make me more radiant; that my quiet weeping
blossom. Oh, how dear you will then be to me, nights,
stricken with grief. Oh that I did not accept you more kneelingly,
inconsolable sisters, did not lose myself more freely
in your loosened hair. We squanderers of pains.
How we look beyond them into the melancholy duration,
whether perhaps they are ending. But in fact they are
our winter-enduring foliage, our dark green of meaning,
one of the times of the hidden year —, not only
time —, they are place, settlement, storehouse, soil, home.

And yet, alas, how strange are the streets of the city of sorrow,
where, in the false stillness made from overpowering sound,
strong, from the casting mold of emptiness, the outflow
boasts: the gilded din, the bursting monument.
Oh, how an angel would stamp out their market place of solace,
bounded by the church, their prefabricated purchase:
clean and closed and disappointed, like a post office on Sunday.
But outside, the edges keep rippling with carnival.
Swings of freedom! Divers and jugglers of zeal!

Und des behübschten Glücks figürliche Schießstatt,   25
wo es zappelt von Ziel und sich blechern benimmt,
wenn ein Geschickterer trifft. Von Beifall zu Zufall
taumelt er weiter; denn Buden jeglicher Neugier
werben, trommeln und plärrn. Für Erwachsene aber
ist noch besonders zu sehn, wie das Geld sich vermehrt, anatomisch, 30
nicht zur Belustigung nur: der Geschlechtsteil des Gelds,
alles, das Ganze, der Vorgang —, das unterrichtet und macht
fruchtbar . . . .
. . . . . Oh aber gleich darüber hinaus,
hinter der letzten Planke, beklebt mit Plakaten des >Todlos<,   35
jenes bitteren Biers, das den Trinkenden süß scheint,
wenn sie immer dazu frische Zerstreuungen kaun . . . ,
gleich im Rücken der Planke, gleich dahinter, ists *wirklich*.
Kinder spielen, und Liebende halten einander, — abseits,
ernst, im ärmlichen Gras, und Hunde haben Natur.   40
Weiter noch zieht es den Jüngling; vielleicht, daß er eine junge
Klage liebt . . . . . Hinter ihr her kommt er in Wiesen. Sie sagt:
— Weit. Wir wohnen dort draußen . . . .

                              Wo? Und der Jüngling
folgt. Ihn rührt ihre Haltung. Die Schulter, der Hals —, vielleicht 45
ist sie von herrlicher Herkunft. Aber er läßt sie, kehrt um,
wendet sich, winkt . . . Was solls? Sie ist eine Klage.

Nur die jungen Toten, im ersten Zustand
zeitlosen Gleichmuts, dem der Entwöhnung,
folgen ihr liebend. Mädchen   50

And the prettified joy of a figured shooting gallery,
that jiggles with targets and clanks tinny
when a more skillful shot hits the mark. From clapping to chancing
he staggers on; for booths of every interest
woo, drum, and blare. For grownups, though, there's still
something special to see, how money breeds, its anatomy,
not just for amusement: money's private parts,
all of it, the whole thing, the act —, that teaches and makes
fruitful . . . .
. . . . . Oh but just beyond that,
behind the last fence, plastered with posters for >Deathless<,
that bitter beer which seems sweet to drinkers
as long as they keep munching fresh distractions with it . . . ,
just in back of the fence, just behind, it is *real*.
Children play and lovers hold one another, — apart,
solemn, in scanty grass, and dogs follow their nature.
But the youth is drawn onward; perhaps because he loves a young
Lament . . . . . He walks behind her and comes into meadows. She says:
— Far. We live out there . . . .

                              Where? And the youth
follows. Her bearing moves him. Her shoulders, her neck —,
perhaps she's of noble descent. But he leaves her, turns around,
gazes back, waves . . . What good is it? She's a Lament.

Only the young dead, in the first phase
of timeless serenity, of being weaned,
follow her lovingly. Girls

wartet sie ab und befreundet sie. Zeigt ihnen leise,
was sie an sich hat. Perlen des Leids und die feinen
Schleier der Duldung. — Mit Jünglingen geht sie
schweigend.

Aber dort, wo sie wohnen, im Tal, der Älteren eine, der Klagen,   55
nimmt sich des Jünglinges an, wenn er fragt: — Wir waren,
sagt sie, ein Großes Geschlecht, einmal, wir Klagen. Die Väter
trieben den Bergbau dort in dem großen Gebirg; bei Menschen
findest du manchmal ein Stück geschliffenes Ur-Leid
oder, aus altem Vulkan, schlackig versteinerten Zorn.   60
Ja, das stammte von dort. Einst waren wir reich. —

Und sie leitet ihn leicht durch die weite Landschaft der Klagen,
zeigt ihm die Säulen der Tempel oder die Trümmer
jener Burgen, von wo Klage-Fürsten das Land
einstens weise beherrscht. Zeigt ihm die hohen   65
Tränenbäume und Felder blühender Wehmut,
(Lebendige kennen sie nur als sanftes Blattwerk);
zeigt ihm die Tiere der Trauer, weidend, — und manchmal
schreckt ein Vogel und zieht, flach ihnen fliegend durchs Aufschaun,
weithin das schriftliche Bild seines vereinsamten Schreis. —   70
Abends führt sie ihn hin zu den Gräbern der Alten
aus dem Klage-Geschlecht, den Sibyllen und Warn-Herrn.
Naht aber Nacht, so wandeln sie leiser, und bald
mondets empor, das über Alles
wachende Grab-Mal. Brüderlich jenem am Nil,   75

78

she waits for, and befriends. Shows them gently
what she's wearing. Pearls of grief and the delicate
veils of forbearance. — With young men she walks
in silence.

But there, where they live, in the valley, one of the older ones,
of the Laments, turns to the youth with kindness: — We were,
she says, a great race, once, we Laments. Our fathers
worked the mines there in the great mountains; among humans
you sometimes find a piece of polished primal sorrow
or, from an old volcano, slaggy petrified wrath.
Yes, that came from there. Once we were rich. —

And she guides him gently through the vast landscape of the Laments,
shows him the columns of the temples or the ruins
of those fortresses from which Lords of Lament
once wisely ruled the land. Shows him the tall
teartrees and fields of blossoming melancholy
(the living know them only as soft foliage);
shows him the animals of mourning, grazing, — and sometimes
a bird takes fright, and flying low through their upward gaze
sketches in the distance the written image of its desolate cry. —
In the evening she leads him to the graves of the
Lament-race elders, the Sibyls and Warning-Lords.
But as night nears, they walk more quietly, and soon,
rising moonlike, watching over
all, the grave-monument. Brother to the one on the Nile,

der erhabene Sphinx —: der verschwiegenen Kammer
Antlitz.
Und sie staunen dem krönlichen Haupt, das für immer,
schweigend, der Menschen Gesicht
auf die Waage der Sterne gelegt.   80

Nicht erfaßt es sein Blick, im Frühtod
schwindelnd. Aber ihr Schaun,
hinter dem Pschent-Rand hervor, scheucht es die Eule. Und sie,
streifend im langsamen Abstrich die Wange entlang,
jene der reifesten Rundung,   85
zeichnet weich in das neue
Totengehör, über ein doppelt
aufgeschlagenes Blatt, den unbeschreiblichen Umriß.

Und höher, die Sterne. Neue. Die Sterne des Leidlands.
Langsam nennt sie die Klage: — Hier,   90
siehe: den *Reiter*, den *Stab*, und das vollere Sternbild
nennen sie: *Fruchtkranz*. Dann, weiter, dem Pol zu:
Wiege; *Weg*; *Das Brennende Buch*; *Puppe*; *Fenster*.
Aber im südlichen Himmel, rein wie im Innern
einer gesegneten Hand, das klar erglänzende *M*,   95
das die Mütter bedeutet . . . . —

Doch der Tote muß fort, und schweigend bringt ihn die ältere
Klage bis an die Talschlucht,
wo es schimmert im Mondschein:

the sublime Sphinx —: the silent, secret chamber's
countenance.
And they marvel at the crowned majestic head, which for all time,
in silence, has laid the human face
on the balance scales of the stars.

His sight doesn't grasp it, still dizzy
with recent death. But their looking
frightens the owl out from behind the crown-rim. And she,
brushing with slow downstrokes along the cheek,
the one with the ripest curve,
sketches softly into the new
hearing of the dead youth, across an opened
double page, the indescribable contour.

And higher, the stars. New ones. The stars of the land of sorrow.
Slowly the Lament names them: — Here,
see: the *Rider*, the *Staff*, and the fuller constellation
they call: *Garland of Fruit*. Then further, toward the pole:
Cradle; Path; The Burning Book; Puppet; Window.
But in the southern sky, pure as in the palm
of a hallowed hand, the clear glowing *M*
signifying the Mothers . . . . —

But the dead youth must go on, and silently the elder
Lament takes him up to the ravine,
shimmering there in the moonlight:

die Quelle der Freude. In Ehrfurcht   100
nennt sie sie, sagt: — Bei den Menschen
ist sie ein tragender Strom. —

Stehn am Fuß des Gebirgs.
Und da umarmt sie ihn, weinend.

Einsam steigt er dahin, in die Berge des Ur-Leids.   105
Und nicht einmal sein Schritt klingt aus dem tonlosen Los.

                                    *

Aber erweckten sie uns, die unendlich Toten, ein Gleichnis,
siehe, sie zeigten vielleicht auf die Kätzchen der leeren
Hasel, die hängenden, oder
meinten den Regen, der fällt auf dunkles Erdreich im Frühjahr. — 110

Und wir, die an *steigendes* Glück
denken, empfänden die Rührung,
die uns beinah bestürzt,
wenn ein Glückliches *fällt*.

the Fountainhead of Joy. With reverence
she names it, says: — Among mankind
it is a sustaining stream. —

They stand at the foot of the mountains.
And there she embraces him, weeping.

In solitude he climbs on, into the mountains of primal sorrow.
And not even his footstep resounds from the soundless fate.

                              *

But if they, the endlessly dead, were to awaken in us an image,
see, they would perhaps point to the catkins of the bare
hazel, hanging down, or
suggest the rain that falls onto the dark soil in spring. —

And we, who think of happiness *rising*,
would feel the emotion
that almost appalls us
when a happy thing *falls*.

Translation Notes

What follows are glimpses into some of the translating principles that have guided our work on the *Duino Elegies*[1], grouped according to various formal dimensions of Rilke's poetry—namely:

Lineation

Throughout the elegies, Rilke takes full advantage of the play of wit made possible by line-end closure. A perfect duplication of his lines

---

[1] The German text is from the 1958 Insel-Verlag edition of *Duineser Elegien*. *Duino* is the name of a castle overlooking the Adriatic Sea, where in 1912 Rilke was the solitary guest of his patroness, the Princess Marie von Thurn und Taxis-Hohenlohe. On a stormy day in January he heard, as if in the wind, the opening line of *The First Elegy*. He completed that elegy within days, and during the remainder of his stay he wrote *The Second Elegy* and parts of others. After the completion of *The Third Elegy* in Paris in 1913 and *The Fourth Elegy* in Munich in 1915, work on the elegies languished until he settled into his "tight castle tower" in Switzerland in 1921. There, in a storm of creativity, Rilke brought the cycle of all ten elegies to completion. *Duineser Elegien* was published in 1923. Rilke died in 1926 at age 51.

in English is of course impossible: German and English differ in syntax and also in the length and rhythm of equivalent words (German *Hoffnung*, for example, is English *hope*). But Rilke's lineation can often be followed precisely, or closely approximated with only minor alterations of his word order—for example, in lines 11 to 13 of *The Ninth Elegy*, by moving three words to a new location (*much* in 9/11 and *us* in 9/12 and 9/13)[2]:

because being here is much, and because apparently	9/11
all that's here needs us, this fleeting world that	9/12
strangely entreats us. Us, the most fleeting.	9/13

Line endings create a break in the poem's onward flow, from strong and decisive stops to barely perceptible pauses. By giving such boundaries to the metrical freedom of the *Duino Elegies*, line-end closures serve as a background against which syllabic rhythms can emerge clearly. And placing a word at the end or the beginning of a line—that is, just before or just after the closure—gives the word a stronger emphasis than it would otherwise have.

The opening of *The Third Elegy* illustrates the value of staying as close as possible to Rilke's lineation:

Eines ist, die Geliebte zu singen. Ein anderes, wehe,	3/1
jenen verborgenen schuldigen Fluß-Gott des Bluts.	3/2
Den sie von weitem erkennt, ihren Jüngling, was weiß er	3/3
selbst von dem Herren der Lust, der aus dem Einsamen oft,	3/4
ehe das Mädchen noch linderte, oft auch als wäre sie nicht,	3/5
ach, von welchem Unkenntlichen triefend, das Gotthaupt	3/6
aufhob, aufrufend die Nacht zu unendlichem Aufruhr.	3/7

---

[2] 9/11 is shorthand for *The Ninth Elegy*, line 11.

It is one thing to sing the beloved. Another, alas,   3/1
to sing that hidden guilty river-god of the blood.   3/2
The one she knows from afar, her young man, what does he know 3/3
himself of the Lord of Lust, who often from his solitude,   3/4
before the girl could soothe, often as though she didn't exist,   3/5
ah, dripping with what unknown, lifted   3/6
his godhead, calling up the night to endless uproar.   3/7

The closure at the end of the first line gives *wehe/alas* an added emphasis; the much stronger stop at the end of the second line, reinforced by the line-end closure, completes the statement of the elegy's theme and clears the way for a long, complex sentence (3/3-7) which takes up a specific instance of the opening theme.

When there are syntactical pauses, as in lines 4, 5, and 7 (indicated here by commas and a period), the line end closure strengthens, or lengthens, the syntactical pause. Sometimes, as in line 3, the closures resist a more insistent onward flow.[3]

Taken one by one, these effects are for the most part subtle, but they are cumulative.

Leitmotif and Theme

By *leitmotif* we mean a word or phrase whose repetition contributes to the development of a theme. When a German word is functioning as a

---

[3] We were unable to come up with a translation that would preserve the word order in lines 6 and 7, so that *Godhead* is not the final word of line 6 as is *Gotthaupt* in the original.

The relative pronoun *der/who* in line 4, introducing a relative clause that is not completed until it reaches *aufhob/lifted* in line 7, begins a suspenseful, forward thrust that is shaped and moderated by the closures of the intervening lines.

leitmotif, we have tried to find an English equivalent that will fit all the contexts where it recurs. *Brauchen/need* is a good example. It first appears near the beginning of *The First Elegy*:

Und so verhalt ich mich denn und verschlucke den Lockruf	1/8
dunkelen Schluchzens. Ach, wen vermögen	1/9
wir denn zu brauchen? Engel nicht, Menschen nicht,	1/10

And so I hold myself back and choke down the alluring call	1/8
of my dark sobbing. Ah then, whom can	1/9
we need? Not angels, not men,	1/10

The question, *Ach, wen vermögen wir denn zu brauchen?/Ah, then whom can we need?* sounds no less peculiar in German than in English. It would be easy to smooth it out—for example, to translate with *Ah, then, to whom can we turn*—but then the bite of Rilke's line, the sense of desperation, would be weakened. More important, *brauchen/need* would be lost as a leitmotif word anchoring its associated theme, one of the most important in the *Duino Elegies*.

This *brauchen/need* theme interweaves the idea of our need with the contrasting idea of our being needed:

Ja, die Frühlinge brauchten dich wohl.	1/26

Yes, the springtimes must have needed you.	1/26

Beginning rather tentatively, the poet ponders whether he is called upon by the springtimes, the stars, his memories, and music—though what he is expected to do for them is not yet clear. His confidence in the idea builds: by line 30 he sees that he has an *Auftrag/mission*. In the course of the elegies this mission clarifies itself, broadening out to include the rest of us humans: "we" are being asked to transform the

88

earth by rendering it into our lived consciousness. The theme
culminates in *The Ninth Elegy:*

Aber weil Hiersein viel ist, und weil uns scheinbar	9/11
alles das Hiesige braucht, dieses Schwindende, das	9/12
seltsam uns angeht. Uns, die Schwindendsten.	9/13

But because being here is much, and because apparently	9/11
all that's here needs us, this fleeting world that	9/12
strangely entreats us. Us, the most fleeting.	9/13

Themes do not, of course, depend solely on leitmotifs, and this one
continues to build in the rest of *The Ninth Elegy* without the
reappearance of *brauchen/need.*[4]

Leitmotif was a primary consideration in our use of *cry* rather than
scream for *schriee* in 1/1. Isolated to the context of the opening passage
of *The First Elegy*, *screamed* is the more appropriate word because of its
emotional intensity and because it matches the harsh sound of the
German. *Screamed* was our first choice.

Wer, wenn ich schriee, hörte mich denn aus der Engel	1/1
Ordnungen?	1/2

Who, if I screamed, would ever hear me among the angels'	1/1
orders?	1/2

---

[4] *brauchen/need* also appears at the end of *The First Elegy.* Line 86 is about our
not being needed—by the young dead. Then, at line 89, the poet again takes
up our needs, this time for the "great mysteries"—the transformative potential
of mourning—especially for the death of a young person.

There are several other occurrences of *brauchen*-related words, whose
relevance to the "need" theme is more remote. They did not lend themselves
to translation that would bring out the continuity of their roots: *Gebräuche/
customs* (1/70); *mein gebrauchtes Gesicht/my worn face* (2/47-48); *der es flächig
verbraucht/gets lost* (5/50); and *verbrauchen/use up* (9/40-41).

But there are two other appearances of the *Schrei* root, and together the three passages form an important leitmotif. For the beautiful, complex image at 10/70, *scream* is clearly inappropriate to the gentle melancholy of the context:

> und manchmal   10/68
> schreckt ein Vogel und zieht, flach ihnen fliegend durchs Aufschaun,
> weithin das schriftliche Bild seines vereinsamten Schreis. —   10/70

> and sometimes   10/68
> a bird takes fright, and flying low through their upward gaze   10/69
> sketches in the distance the written image of its desolate cry. —   10/70

And *scream/screamed* would be impossible for *Schrei* (*-es*) and *schrie* (*-est*) at 7/2, where the bird's call is likened to the poet's voice, in this case his appeal to a beloved:

> Werbung nicht mehr, nicht Werbung, entwachsene Stimme,   7/1
> sei deines Schreies Natur; zwar schrieest du rein wie der Vogel,   7/2
> wenn ihn die Jahreszeit aufhebt, die steigende, beinah vergessend,   7/3
> daß er ein kümmerndes Tier und nicht nur ein einzelnes Herz sei,   7/4
> das sie ins Heitere wirft, in die innigen Himmel.   7/5

> Wooing no more, not wooing, outgrown voice,   7/1
> be the nature of your cry; although you cried purely like the bird   7/2
> when the season — the ascending one — lifts him up, almost forgetting
> that he's a troubled animal and not just a single heart   7/4
> flung into brightness, into the tender skies.   7/5

Finally, preserving in English the *Schrei* leitmotif respects Rilke's association of angels with birds, most prominently at 2/1-3:

> Jeder Engel ist schrecklich. Und dennoch, weh mir,   2/1
> ansing ich euch, fast tödliche Vögel der Seele,   2/2
> wissend um euch.   2/3

90

Every angel is terrible. And yet, alas,   2/1
I sing unto you, almost deadly birds of the soul,   2/2
knowing about you.   2/3

The *Vogel/bird* leitmotif extends more mutedly this association of *Schrei/ cry* with birds.[5]

World-space is a somewhat awkward neologism, but we found that only a literal translation of the leitmotif *Weltraum* would render the complexity of Rilke's choice. *Welt/world and Raum/space* occur frequently throughout the elegies.[6] *Weltraum* occurs three times:

O und die Nacht, die Nacht, wenn der Wind voller Weltraum   1/18
uns am Angesicht zehrt —,   1/19

Oh and the night, the night, when the wind full of world-space   1/18
gnaws on our faces —,   1/19

Schmeckt denn der Weltraum,   2/29
in den wir uns lösen, nach uns? Fangen die Engel   2/30
wirklich nur Ihriges auf, ihnen Entströmtes,   2/31
oder ist manchmal, wie aus Versehen, ein wenig   2/32
unseres Wesens dabei?   2/33

---

[5] The *Vogel/bird* leitmotif appears at 1/24, 2/2, 4/3, 8/56, and 10/69-70.
Other leitmotif words include:
 bleiben/stay (1/13, 1/15, 1/17, 1/19, 1/35/ 1/53, 7/91, 8/53, 9/52. (9/52
was better translated as *goes on)*;
atmen/breathe, atmend/breathing and *Atem/breath* (1/24, 2/19, 7/24, 7/37-38,
8/18).

[6] Aside from these three instances of *Weltraum, Welt* appears at 1/13, 3/28,
4/73, 6/26, 6/38 (twice), 7/50, 7/63, 8/16, 8/28; and at 5/10 and 9/54 as
Weltall. Raum appears at 1/77, 1/93, 4/50, 8/15, and 8/59; at 3/33 as
menschlichern Raum; at 3/33 as *Nacht-Raum)*; and at 4/73 as *Zwischenraum.*

Does then world-space taste of us   2/29
when we dissolve in it? Do the angels really capture   2/30
only what's theirs, their outstreamed radiance,   2/31
or is sometimes, as though by mistake, a little   2/32
of our essence in it?   2/33

Und ihr, hab ich nicht recht,   4/47
die ihr mich liebtet für den kleinen Anfang   4/48
Liebe zu euch, von dem ich immer abkam,   4/49
weil mir der Raum in eurem Angesicht,   4/50
da ich ihn liebte, überging in Weltraum,   4/51
in dem ihr nicht mehr wart   4/52

And all you, am I not right,   4/47
you who loved me for my slight beginning   4/48
of love for you, from which I always strayed   4/49
because for me the space in your features,   4/50
since I loved it, turned into world-space   4/51
where you no longer were.   4/52

Weltraum is the ordinary German word for outer space, but Rilke uses it
in a more spiritual sense, close to *das Offene/the Open* and *All/All.*[7] But
between its two parts, *Welt* and *Raum*, there is also an element of
contradiction which is explicit in lines 8/15-16:

Wir haben nie, nicht einen einzigen Tag,   8/14
den reinen Raum vor uns, in den die Blumen   8/15
unendlich aufgehn. Immer ist es Welt   8/16
und niemals Nirgends ohne Nicht: das Reine,   8/17
Unüberwachte, das man atmet und   8/18
unendlich *weiß* und nicht begehrt. Als Kind   8/19
verliert sich eins im Stilln an dies und wird   8/20
gerüttelt. Oder jener stirbt und *ists.*   8/21

---

[7] Das Offene appears at 8/2 and 8/8—and in different but related senses at
5/61, 7/42, and 8/91-92. *All/All* appears at 9/41-42.

Denn nah am Tod sieht man den Tod nicht mehr   8/22
und starrt *hinaus*, vielleicht mit großem Tierblick.   8/23

We never have, not for a single day,   8/14
the pure space before us into which the flowers   8/15
endlessly unfold. Always it is world   8/16
and never Nowhere without Not: the pure,   8/17
the unwatched, that one breathes and   8/18
infinitely *knows* and does not covet. As a child   8/19
one gets lost there in the silence and is   8/20
shaken back. Or someone dies and so *becomes it.*   8/21
For near to death, one sees death no longer   8/22
and stares *out*, perhaps with the wide animal gaze.   8/23

Rilke uses *Raum* here (8/15) to enrich an idea introduced a few lines earlier, at the opening of *The Eighth Elegy*, where he uses instead the word *Offene/Open*. *Raum* is *das Reine/the pure*; it is *niemals Nirgends ohne Nicht/never Nowhere without Not*, and one knows it *unendlich/infinitely*. *Welt/ world* (8/16), on the other hand, stands in opposition as the chaotic, busy, perverse world of ordinary human consciousness. Though on the surface *Weltraum* refers to the infinite spiritual realm, the word at the same time contains this tension of conflicting parts.

Welt and *Raum* are both also used in ways that then contradict themselves. In *The Seventh Elegy*, for example, *Welt* is *innen/within* and a few lines later is characterized as *dumpfe/dull and heavy*:

Nirgends, Geliebte, wird Welt sein, als innen.   7/50

Nowhere, beloved, will world be but within.   7/50

Jede dumpfe Umkehr der Welt hat solche Enterbte   7/63

Each dull, heavy turn of the world has such disinherited ones   7/63

93

Throughout the elegies, in differing appearances of *Welt* and *Raum* as well as of *Weltraum*, the richness of this play of opposition develops until it climaxes in *The Eighth Elegy*.

Ambiguity and Context

Where Rilke's wording is ambiguous, a careful consideration of the context can shed light on the difficulty. Lines 1-4 of *The Eighth Elegy* are an instance:

Mit allen Augen sieht die Kreatur	8/1
das Offene. Nur unsre Augen sind	8/2
wie umgekehrt und ganz um sie gestellt	8/3
als Fallen, rings um ihren freien Ausgang.	8/4

With all its eyes the creature sees	8/1
the Open. Only our eyes are	8/2
as though reversed, and placed all around them	8/3
as traps, encircling their free exit.	8/4

The antecedent of both *sie* in line 3 and *ihren* in line 4 is not clear. In German the singular of the personal pronoun *sie* is identical to its plural, so it might be translated either as *it* or as *them*; similarly, the possessive pronoun *ihren* may be translated here either as *its* or as *their*. Both *sie* and *ihren* may refer, then, (if singular) to the feminine noun *die Kreatur/the creature* (8/1) or (if plural) to *unsre Augen/our eyes* (8/2) or, by implication, to *allen Augen/all its eyes* (8/1)[8]

Taking *sie* and *ihren* as singular feminine (referring therefore to the feminine noun *die Kreatur/the creature*), limits the English to a single

---

[8] Though *Augen* in line 1 may not strictly speaking be regarded as a referent, it is one by association.

94

meaning: our eyes are placed around the creature's eyes, that is, the animals' eyes, trapping them into our kind of consciousness:

With all its eyes the creature sees	8/1
the Open. Only our eyes are	8/2
as though reversed, and placed all around it [her]	8/3
as traps, encircling its [her] free exit.	8/4

Taking *sie* and *ihren* as plural, the translation is as we have it:

With all its eyes the creature sees	8/1
the Open. Only our eyes are	8/2
as though reversed, and placed all around them	8/3
as traps, encircling their free exit.	8/4

In English, as against German, one cannot take these pronouns as both singular and plural. A translator must choose. If *sie* and *ihren* are taken as plural, as we have done, the ambiguity remains: *sie* and *ihren* may refer either to *unsre Augen/our eyes* or to *allen Augen/all its eyes*. If they refer to *allen Augen/all its eyes*, then the meaning is identical to what it would be if the pronouns were singular: we force our kind of consciousness on the animals.

The most puzzling of the possibilities—that our eyes are traps for themselves—is supported strongly by the context. As the poem continues, it does not claim that human consciousness challenges the animals' direct contact with *das Offene/the Open*, but, on the contrary, insists that animals remain in contact with it—with *Weltraum/world-space* —while human consciousness sees only *Gestaltung/form*, having been turned *rückwärts/backward* in childhood.

Was draußen *ist*, wir wissens aus des Tiers	8/5
Antlitz allein; denn schon das frühe Kind	8/6

wenden wir um und zwingens, daß es rückwärts 8/7
Gestaltung sehe, nicht das Offne, das 8/8
im Tiergesicht so tief ist. Frei von Tod. 8/9
Ihn sehen wir allein; das freie Tier 8/10
hat seinen Untergang stets hinter sich 8/11
und vor sich Gott, und wenn es geht, so gehts 8/12
in Ewigkeit, so wie die Brunnen gehen. 8/13

What *is* outside we know only from the animal's 8/5
countenance; for already we turn around 8/6
the young child and force it to see backwards, 8/7
see form, not the Open that's 8/8
so deep in the animal face. Free of death— 8/9
it, only we see. The free animal 8/10
has its demise always behind it 8/11
and before it God, and when it moves, it moves 8/12
in eternity, as the fountains move. 8/13

In lines 35-42, this comparison is developed further:

Wäre Bewußtheit unsrer Art in dem 8/35
sicheren Tier, das uns entgegenzieht 8/36
in anderer Richtung —, riß es uns herum 8/37
mit seinem Wandel. Doch sein Sein ist ihm 8/38
unendlich, ungefaßt und ohne Blick 8/39
auf seinen Zustand, rein, so wie sein Ausblick. 8/40
Und wo wir Zukunft sehn, dort sieht es Alles 8/41
und sich in Allem und geheilt für immer. 8/42

Were consciousness of our kind in the 8/35
sure animal that moves toward us 8/36
in the other direction —, it would spin us around 8/37
with its transformation. But to it, its being is 8/38
unending, ungrasped and without a glance 8/39
at its condition, pure, like its outward gaze. 8/40
And where we see the future, there it sees All 8/41
and itself in All and healed forever. 8/42

Translating *sie* and *ihren* as plural retains the puzzling dual
possibilities for their meaning; translating them as singular, while

96

presenting a clear, straightforward English text, eliminates what we take to be the more likely interpretation. Did Rilke mean that our eyes are surrounded and trapped by themselves, as it were, or that our eyes are surrounding and trapping the animals' eyes and preventing their "free exit?" Or did he intend that the seemingly ambiguous reference of the pronouns leave the question open?

Respect for Rilke's wording has, we hope—despite the difficulty it presents for the reader of English—rendered a text that is as close as possible to what Rilke actually wrote. It gives readers the opportunity to work out their own understanding of what the text means.

Lines 82-85 of *The First Elegy* also illustrate the importance of keeping the context in mind. The verb *übertönt* appears in line 1/85. We have translated it as *overpowers*.

Engel (sagt man) wüßten oft nicht, ob sie unter	1/82
Lebenden gehn oder Toten. Die ewige Strömung	1/83
reißt durch beide Bereiche alle Alter	1/84
immer mit sich und übertönt sie in beiden.	1/85
Angels (they say) often don't know if they're walking	1/82
among the living or the dead. The eternal current	1/83
through both domains sweeps all ages	1/84
along with it forever, and overpowers them in both.	1/85

The almost inevitable English equivalent for *übertönt* in line 85 is *drown out*: one sound overpowers another. But the preceding expression, *die ewige Strömung/the eternal current* may lead some English readers to take *drown out* literally—simply as *drowns,* or at least to hear in the back of the mind this implication which is absent from the German. That misunderstanding would alter the meaning of the eternal current—so that it would not only carry the living and the dead with it, but submerge them.[9]

Unorthodox Constructions

At the opening of *The Seventh Elegy* the poet makes a strong demand on himself:

Werbung nicht mehr, nicht Werbung, entwachsene Stimme,	7/1
sei deines Schreies Natur	7/2

Wooing no more, not wooing, outgrown voice,	7/1
be the nature of your cry	7/2

At the end of the elegy, triumphantly addressing the angel, he praises human accomplishments in creating "these giving, these *our* spaces" (lines 78-79), concluding with

Doch selbst nur	7/83
eine Liebende —, oh, allein am nächtlichen Fenster . . . ,	7/84
reichte sie dir nicht ans Knie —?	7/85

But even	7/83
just one woman in love —, oh, alone at the window by night . . . ,	7/84
did she not come up to your knee — ?	7/85

Then comes a surprising shift in tone, reinforced through syntax,

---

[9] Lines 37-40 of *The Fifth Elegy* are another instance of Rilke's ambiguous wording and obscure referents.

voice, punctuation, and typography:[10]

> Glaub *nicht,* daß ich werbe. 7/86
> Engel, und würb ich dich auch! Du kommst nicht. 7/87

> *Don't* think I'm wooing. 7/86
> Angel, and even if I wooed you! You don't come. 7/87

Given the subjunctive verb of the first, hypothetical, clause in line 87 (*und würb ich dich auch!/and even if I wooed you!*), one expects the sentence to flow to a concluding subjunctive clause, separated from the first by a comma:

> Glaub *nicht* daß ich werbe.
> Engel, und würb ich dich auch, du kämst nicht.

> *Don't* think I'm wooing.
> Angel, and even if I wooed you, you wouldn't come

Instead, the subjunctive, hypothetical first clause is followed by an indicative conclusion. The two clauses are separated decisively by an exclamation point, leaving the hypothetical first clause hanging as a sentence fragment and the indicative final clause standing starkly alone as a statement of hard fact.

We take Rilke's disjunct structure to be an indication of strong emotion, reflecting a sudden change in the poet's relationship to the angel. Whatever one's interpretation, the structure of the passage is well worth preserving in translation. Rendering it precisely gives readers of English the opportunity to come to their own conclusion

---

[10] This shift is emphasized by a typographical strategy used occasionally throughout the elegies and well worth preserving in translation: line 86 begins a new line directly under the end of line 85. See *Subdivisions* below.

about this moment in the elegy.

Flavoring Particles

Flavoring particles like *denn* in the first line of *The First Elegy*, which we have translated with *ever*, are notoriously slippery for translators:

> Wer, wenn ich schriee, hörte mich denn aus der Engel / Ordnungen?

> Who, if I cried out, would ever hear me among the angels' / orders?

Sometimes it seems best not to carry them over at all into English, but *denn* in this instance imparts a nuance that is evoked by *ever*: a lightly-touched ironic, nearly despairing, certainty that the poet's outcry will not bring a response.

wohl (1/26), which we have rendered with *must have*, is another example of a flavoring particle.

Punctuation, Rhythm, and Syntax

Punctuation notates rhythm as well as meaning. In lines 41-58 of *The Fifth Elegy*—and in general throughout the elegies—we have been able to translate Rilke's punctuation—and therefore to some extent his rhythm— into English because we have, in large part, duplicated his lineation and syntax.

Du, der mit dem Aufschlag,	5/41
wie nur Früchte ihn kennen, unreif,	5/42
täglich hundertmal abfällt vom Baum der gemeinsam	5/43

erbauten Bewegung (der, rascher als Wasser, in wenig	5/44
Minuten Lenz, Sommer und Herbst hat) —	5/45
abfällt und anprallt ans Grab:	5/46
manchmal, in halber Pause, will dir ein liebes	5/47
Antlitz entstehn hinüber zu deiner selten	5/48
zärtlichen Mutter; doch an deinen Körper verliert sich,	5/49
der es flächig verbraucht, das schüchtern	5/50
kaum versuchte Gesicht . . . Und wieder	5/51
klatscht der Mann in die Hand zu dem Ansprung, und eh dir	5/52
jemals ein Schmerz deutlicher wird in der Nähe des immer	5/53
trabenden Herzens, kommt das Brennen der Fußsohln	5/54
ihm, seinem Ursprung, zuvor mit ein paar dir	5/55
rasch in die Augen gejagten leiblichen Tränen.	5/56
Und dennoch, blindlings,	5/57
das Lächeln	5/58

You, who with the impact	5/41
known only to fruit, unripe,	5/42
fall a hundred times a day from the tree of mutually	5/43
built movement (which quicker than water, in a few	5/44
minutes has spring, summer, and autumn) —	5/45
fall off and crash against the grave:	5/46
sometimes, in a half-pause, a loving look	5/47
wants to emerge toward your seldom	5/48
tender mother; but that shy,	5/49
scarcely attempted face gets lost	5/50
on your body's surface . . . And again	5/51
the man claps his hands for another leap, and always	5/52
before the pain can get clearer around your ever-	5/53
trotting heart, the burning of your soles	5/54
anticipates it, its origin, with a few bodily tears	5/55
quickly chased into your eyes.	5/56
And nevertheless, blindly,	5/57
the smile	5/58

Here are some of the details of the interplay between syntax, rhythm, and punctuation:

In line 42, the adjective *unreif/unripe* is given special emphasis by being separated from its subject and placed at the end of the line, set off by commas.

By isolating the seasonal metaphor in lines 44-45, the parenthesis encourages readers to dwell for a moment on the static tree image before going on to the breathless pace of the seasonal images racing by faster than water. The combination of the long dash with the line ending adds an extra "beat."

The colon at the end of line 46 maintains the momentum of the sentence as the boy is hurried from one stage of the act to another.[11]

The semicolon in line 49 does not simply reinforce the syntactical enjambment, but throws the energy forward into the next clause.

The ellipsis in line 51, by commanding pause and attention, reverberates with the young acrobat's poignant plight. In particular his attempted glance (a smile coming from his heart) is aborted by the clap and then intercepted by the performers' mask-like smile, which emerges during the five ellipsis points of

---

[11] Many other passages that employ colons lend themselves to meticulous translation: lines 39-42 and 54-58 of *The First Elegy*, for example. Rilke also uses some unique punctuation marks: long or short dashes followed or preceded by a comma, semicolon, colon, or by ellipsis points. Since these are distinctive elements of Rilke's craft, we have tried to include them in the translation. (We have followed the 1958 Inselverlag edition of the German text.)

102

line 58 and the blank line that follows.[12]

Subdivisions

The elegies employ a variety of formats for division into parts. We have rendered them precisely:

blank lines between parts: a fresh start;

small indentations: a less distinct separation, sometimes following a blank line;

deep indentations: lines that begin directly below the end of the preceding line. This odd punctuation is scattered through the elegies. In every case but one (10/43-4) what follows the indentation is a short sentence, an independent clause, or (in the case of >Subrisio Saltat<, 5/62-3) a single, condensed idea; and these compact texts are emphasized by their typographical isolation and an intensified (vertical) relationship to the preceding line.

To give an example (6/8-9) in context:

Feigenbaum, seit wie lange schon ists mir bedeutend,	6/1
wie du die Blüte beinah ganz überschlägst	6/2
und hinein in die zeitig entschlossene Frucht,	6/3
ungerühmt, drängst dein reines Geheimnis.	6/4
Wie der Fontäne Rohr treibt dein gebognes Gezweig	6/5

---

[12] We have followed Rilke's practice of varying the number of ellipsis points, from three to ten, evidently to suggest different degrees and qualities of juncture or closure. Line 5/51, for example, has three dots, line 5/58 has five.

abwärts den Saft und hinan: und er springt aus dem Schlaf,   6/6
fast nicht erwachend, ins Glück seiner süßesten Leistung.   6/7
Sieh: wie der Gott in den Schwan.   6/8
      ...... Wir aber verweilen, 6/9
ach, uns rühmt es zu blühn, und ins verspätete Innre   6/10
unserer endlichen Frucht gehn wir verraten hinein.   6/11

Fig tree, for how long now has it been meaningful to me   6/1
the way you almost completely bypass flowering   6/2
and into the early-determined fruit,   6/3
unpraised, urge your pure secret.   6/4
Like the fountain's pipe your curved branches drive   6/5
the sap downward and up: and it springs from sleep,   6/6
almost without awakening, into the joy of its sweetest achievement.
See: like the god into the swan.   6/8
      ...... But we linger,   6/9
ah, our pride is in blossoming, and we enter   6/10
the delayed interior of our final fruit betrayed.   6/11

The punctuation of lines 8 and 9 has a distinct effect on "......
Wir aber verweilen/ ...... *But we linger:*" the ellipsis, itself a
lingering over the transition from line 8 to line 9, slows the pace
and thereby reinforces the singularity of line 9. At the same time,
the vertical alignment of the two ideas ties them together more
emphatically. This is subtle—and a depth dimension worth
capturing for the English reader.[13]

---

[13] Other instances of deep indentation occur at:
    3/84-5:   *Verhalt ihn ...... /Hold him back* ......
    5/12-13: *Und kaum dort/And scarcely there*
    5/62-3:   *>Subrisio Saltat<*
    7/85-6:   *Glaub nicht, daß ich werbe./Don't think I'm wooing.*
    9/6-7:   *Oh, nicht, weil Glück ist/Oh not because happiness is*
    10/43-4: *Wo? Und der Jüngling/Where? And the youth*

Translating vs. Interpreting

The *Duino Elegies* are at times monumental, dark, and majestic, at other times luminous and vibrant, sparkling with gayety and irony. They are everywhere subtle, passionate, and provocative. We have resisted the temptation to smooth the path when this rich creativity results in paradoxical or idiosyncratic constructions, which are an integral part of Rilke's poetic language. As *The First Elegy* says, in lines 30-31:

> Das alles war Auftrag.
> Aber bewältigtest du's?

> All that was a mission.
> But did you accomplish it?

We hope so.

Made in the USA
San Bernardino, CA
06 December 2015